"Mark Jones's helpful discussion of
tian faith demonstrates his point, sha
resources for devotion to Christ are fo
tigation conducted under the authority ᴏ ᴊᴄ ı ɪᴘᴛ ᴜ ɪᴇ.

Robert Letham, Professor of Systematic and Historical Theology,
Union School of Theology

"If you are to experience vitality and growth in the Christian life, nothing
is more important than using a spiritual compass oriented to true north.
In this book, Mark Jones puts such a compass in our hands. The Christian
faith is about living for God! I wish such a book had been put in my hands
when I came to faith in Christ. Here is a book to read and pass on to young
believers so that they can use rightly calibrated spiritual compasses from
the get-go!"

Conrad Mbewe, Pastor, Kabwata Baptist Church; Chancellor,
African Christian University, Lusaka, Zambia

"Primers like this—a trenchant reminder of the vital matters that lie at
the heart of the Christian faith—are ever needful, and especially so in this
theologically befuddled generation that is far too often heedless of the
value of the past. Highly recommended!"

Michael A. G. Haykin, Professor of Church History and Biblical
Spirituality, The Southern Baptist Theological Seminary

"Nothing could be more important than getting a right understanding of
the Christian faith. Mark Jones's *Living for God* elegantly and accurately
presents five pillars fundamental to Christianity. Summarizing the Bible's
teaching with key concepts from the Reformed tradition, this book is not
too big and not too small. Jones writes with the broad and deep knowledge
of a scholar and the care and maturity of an experienced pastor. His book
will be useful both as a starting point for the new Christian and as a point
to which the mature can return. I look forward to sharing it with friends
and family."

Emily Van Dixhoorn, author, *Confessing the Faith Study Guide*

Living for God

A Short Introduction to
the Christian Faith

Mark Jones

CROSSWAY®

WHEATON, ILLINOIS

Cover design and illustration: Jorge Canedo Estrada

First printing 2020

Printed in the United States of America

Trade paperback ISBN: 978-1-4335-6625-7
ePub ISBN: 978-1-4335-6628-8
PDF ISBN: 978-1-4335-6626-4
Mobipocket ISBN: 978-1-4335-6627-1

Library of Congress Cataloging-in-Publication Data

Names: Jones, Mark, 1980– author.
Title: Living for God : a short introduction to the Christian faith / Mark Jones.
Description: Wheaton : Crossway, 2020. | Includes bibliographical references and index.
Identifiers: LCCN 2019014550 (print) | ISBN 9781433566257 (tp)
Subjects: LCSH: Reformed Church—Doctrines. | Theology, Doctrinal. | Christian life—Reformed authors.
Classification: LCC BX9422.3 .J66 2020 (print) | LCC BX9422.3 (ebook) | DDC 230—dc23
LC record available at https://lccn.loc.gov/2019014550
LC ebook record available at https://lccn.loc.gov/2019980349

Crossway is a publishing ministry of Good News Publishers.

VP		29	28	27	26	25	24	23	22	21	20
15	14	13	12	11	10	9	8	7	6	5	4	3	2	1

To all my Facebook friends, who have encouraged
me in my ministry with their "likes."

I, as a believer that Jesus of Nazareth, a Jew, the Christ of the Greeks, was the Anointed One of God (born of the seed of David . . .), am grafted onto the true vine, and am one of the heirs of God's covenant with Israel. . . . I'm a Christian. . . . Don't put me in another box.

—Johnny Cash, *Man in White*

Contents

Acknowledgments

I would like to express my thanks to Justin Taylor and the Crossway team, including my editor, David Barshinger, for bringing this book to publication. They continue to make books better through their hard work and expertise. Two friends of mine deserve special mention for offering some good advice along the way: Bob McKelvey and Garry Vanderveen. Faith Vancouver Presbyterian Church, where I have happily served for over twelve years now, has not only allowed me to write but also encouraged me to write and serve the kingdom in various ways. I owe a great deal to my wife and children, who also support me constantly.

As a pastor, I've wanted to be able to hand out a book on the basics of the Christian faith. The triune God has given me the privilege of writing such a book myself, something I count as a great blessing. All praise to the Father, Son, and Holy Spirit for whatever good may come from this volume.

Introduction

Living for God

From all this it follows that theology is most correctly defined as the doctrine of living for God through Christ.
—Petrus van Mastricht

Theology is the doctrine or teaching of living to God.
—William Ames

Living for God. True living is when we live for God: "For now we live, if you are standing fast in the Lord" (1 Thess. 3:8). We either live for ourselves, with the many manifestations of that lifestyle, or we live for God, with the many manifestations of that lifestyle. Living for God in this life means living for God in the life to come. To enjoy the latter, we must engage in the former.

So how do we live for God? Christianity explains *how* in the best and only way possible.

Our approach to the Christian life must be grounded in the conviction that sound doctrine and godly living go hand in hand, with the former providing the foundation for the latter. Paul understood this clearly when he exhorted his pastoral protégé Timothy in a context affected by false teaching and ungodly living: "Keep a close watch on yourself and on the teaching. Persist in this, for by so doing you will save both yourself and your hearers" (1 Tim. 4:16). We could go on with other examples, but you may observe in the letters of Paul, especially Romans and Ephesians, that doctrine and life are inextricably linked (i.e., the indicatives lead to imperatives).

C. S. Lewis also understood the intimate relationship between theology and ethics. For example, in *Mere Christianity* he first sets forth teachings that are fundamental to Christianity and then moves on to discuss the morality that emerges from such theological principles. Elsewhere, Lewis makes this connection explicitly:

> For my own part, I tend to find the doctrinal books often more helpful in devotion than the devotional books, and I rather suspect that the same experience may await others. I believe that many who find that "nothing happens" when they sit down, or kneel down, to a book of devotion, would find that the heart sings unbidden while they are working their way through a tough bit of theology with a pipe in their teeth and a pencil in their hand.[1]

In other words, a truly devotional book will be doctrinal, but a doctrinal book should also inspire devotion. Doctrine and devotion are friends (Rom. 11:33–36).

With such a link in mind, the Puritan William Ames famously affirmed, "Theology is the doctrine or teaching of living to God."[2] For Ames, theology, as conceptual as it will always be within the mind, must never be divorced from the practical response that issues forth according to the will. The Dutch Reformed theologian Petrus van Mastricht built on Ames to claim, "Theology is most correctly defined as the doctrine of living for God through Christ."[3] The addition "through Christ" rightly emphasizes the fact that living for and to God remains impossible apart from our union with Christ. Like Ames, van Mastricht believed that theory and practice go together in theology, and so, "Nothing is offered in theology that does not incline to this point, namely, that a person's life should be directed toward God. . . . Therefore theology is nothing other than the doctrine of living for God through Christ."[4] As a result, good theology (that which is well received) results in good living (that which is well delivered).

Mere Christianity

I hope these thoughts help explain why a book on the Christian life comes in such a doctrinal form. You may also note that I focus on only five teachings: the Trinity, Christ, the Spirit, the church, and life after death. I chose these as principal doctrines that define Christianity at its very foundation. In consideration of this choice, let's come back to Lewis's *Mere Christianity*. In speaking of "mere Christianity," Lewis denotes an essential faith that unites all true believers, and he admits to borrowing the title and the understanding from the Puritan Richard Baxter.

Baxter spoke against the sectarian tendencies of denominations by referring to himself as "a Meer Christian" of the "Christian Church" of all ages and places. In line with mere Christianity, he called himself a "Catholic Christian," not in the sense of the church of Rome but in the sense of being universally in line with the common affirmations of the Apostles' Creed. It was to "that Party which is so against Parties" that he belonged rather than to "any dividing or contentious Sect."[5]

We might conclude that Baxter unfairly maligns denominational convictions to view himself as a mere Christian. Likewise, we might not agree with how he fleshes out what constitutes a mere Christian. Still, his "Meer Christian[ity]" hits home as he longs for a common ground that unites all true believers. This must not be seen as a path of compromise or ease for Baxter but as a road that disdains unnecessary division. Regarding different Christian sects, he had earlier maintained,

> It is easy to be of any one of these parties; but to be a Christian, which all pretend to, is not so easy. It is easy to have a burning zeal for any divided party or cause, but the common zeal for Christian Religion, is not so easy to be kindled, or kept alive, but requires as much diligence to maintain it, as dividing zeal requires to quench it. It is easy to love a party as a party; but to keep up Catholick charity to all Christians, and to live in that holy love and converse, which is requisite to a Christian communion of Saints, is not so easy.[6]

Within such a communion exist "all that be holy in the world," claims Baxter, obviously with a view of living for God through Christ. It follows, then, that this communion should "live as those that believe that there is a life everlasting, where the Sanctified shall live in endless joy, and the unsanctified in endless punishment and woe; live but as men that verily believe a Heaven and a Hell, and a Day of Judgment."[7]

Obviously, not all who would consider themselves "mere Christians" can rightly lay claim to the title. The seventeenth-century heretic John Biddle called himself a "mere Christian," only to be refuted (as commissioned by Parliament) by John Owen, who observed, "And now, whether this man be a 'mere Christian' or a mere Lucian, let the reader judge."[8] Like Biddle, many today would claim the title "mere Christians" but pay only lip service to or even openly deny truths foundational to the Christian faith, such as the eternality of Jesus Christ as the second person of the Trinity.

I must confess my dependence here on Baxter and Lewis and their focus on "mere Christianity." With this in mind, this book has as its primary goal to set forth foundational or principal truths of the Christian faith and so explain what living for God and to God entails. To put it another way, this book represents what I, as a pastor, would like to offer my flock and other Christians as an "introduction to the Christian faith."

This approach finds its historical friend in the Apostles' Creed, which many have discoursed on throughout church history as they have set forth the basics of the Christian faith. Even in his *Institutes of Elenctic Theology*—a highly sophisticated and detailed systematic theology written in the seventeenth century—Francis Turretin speaks of the fundamental articles of the faith as

> the doctrines concerning the sacred Scriptures as inspired
> . . . being the only and perfect rule of faith; concerning the
> unity of God and the Trinity; concerning Christ, the Re-
> deemer, and his most perfect satisfaction; concerning sin
> and its penalty—death; concerning the law and its inability
> to save; concerning justification by faith; concerning the
> necessity of grace and good works, sanctification and the
> worship of God, the church, the resurrection of the dead,
> the final judgment and eternal life and such as are connected
> with these. All these are so strictly joined together that they
> mutually depend on each other. One cannot be withdrawn
> without overthrowing all the rest.[9]

Besides Turretin, many authors have summarized principal doctrines of the Christian faith. Whether from the Reformation and post-Reformation periods or in the last few hundred years, many of these works have much to commend to them. But emphases shift from writer to writer. I have my own thoughts on basic Christianity, which I claim stresses the following five foundational pillars. Put simply, the Christian faith is defined as that which is

1. Trinity oriented
2. Christ focused
3. Spirit energized
4. Church inhabited
5. Heaven anticipated

You may notice that I have deliberately chosen to set forth doctrines that we do not simply believe but that we respond to in faith. So, for example, to truly believe in the Trinity is to *orient* our lives around communion with the one God in three persons—hence, it is "Trinity oriented." With this in mind, I can make use of the five pillars above to offer this expanded definition of theology:

> Theology is the doctrine of living unto God, through Christ, by the Spirit, in the context of the church, and with a view to the glories of heaven.

Using these five pillars more explicitly, we could rightly affirm,

> Theology is the doctrine of living unto God through a Trinity-oriented, Christ-focused, Spirit-energized, church-inhabited, and heaven-anticipated life.

This definition gives us a short summary of the five pillars highlighted above. If Christian theology does not lead us to the God who revealed it, then it is neither truly Christian nor truly theological. So churches where the worship, teaching, and preaching fail to promote living for God through Christ by the Spirit are dangerous places, since many feel all is well when the opposite is true. Likewise, the emotions stirred up in some worship services do not necessarily constitute such life, which must find its expression (albeit imperfectly in this world) in all of life. This is strong language, but who wants to waste their time worshiping in a context where they are regressing spiritually, where falsehood displaces the truth, where God is created in the image of man, or where entertainment has replaced "reverence and awe" (Heb. 12:28)?

Scripture-Grounded Life

Some may argue—especially with the Turretin quote above, which starts theology with God's word—that I have missed another pillar. Should we not speak of a Scripture-grounded life as well? Indeed, we agree that any discussion of the Trinity, Christ, the Spirit, the church, or heaven demands a foundational source revealed outside ourselves by God alone, who, by condescending to our limitations as humans, made himself as Creator known to us as creatures.

I write to set forth principal teachings unto life as revealed in the word of God alone. Without the Reformation conviction of *sola Scriptura*, this book would in vain seek to promote living for God.

We serve a God who in mercy has chosen to reveal himself as Creator to his creatures. He reveals himself clearly to all humanity in creation and in the heart of created man himself. Though God has made himself plain to all mankind, so that we are "without excuse," men in their ungodliness "suppress the truth" (Rom. 1:18–20). Thus, while this natural revelation is enough to show God clearly, for fallen man it is no longer sufficient to give us life unto God.

We therefore need the special revelation permanently recorded in Scripture to overcome our sin and lead us back to God through Christ, who alone, as the God-man, can reconcile us to God. The Westminster Larger Catechism (1647) summarizes this thinking quite well in the answer to the second question:

> Q: How does it appear that there is a God?
> A: The very light of nature in man, and the works of God, declare plainly that there is a God; but his word and Spirit only do sufficiently and effectually reveal him unto men for their salvation.[10]

So while we can know God through the light of nature, we come to him through Christ only by the light of special revelation. As the Westminster Confession of Faith makes clear, the embrace of such revelation demands "the inward illumination of the Spirit of God" (1.6) for the "saving understanding" of what he reveals (e.g., 1 Thess. 1:5).

This word comes from God as that which "is breathed out" by him, the very inspired (and thus inerrant) word of God, and so it is "profitable for teaching, for reproof, for correction, and for training in righteousness" (2 Tim. 3:16). Did you notice that Paul says that the word is useful for teaching (doctrine) and training (life)? Indeed, van Mastricht defends his definition of theology as "living unto God through Christ" from Scripture, which denotes theology as the "words of eternal life" (John 6:68; cf. Acts 5:20) and identifies anyone who has "learned from the Father" as the same as the one who "comes" to Christ (John 6:45). "The entirety of this theology," argues van Mastricht, "is occupied in forming the life of a person and directing it toward God insofar as everything encountered in the Scriptures flows together and aims at this end."[11]

The Westminster Confession of Faith's first chapter remains one of the best brief statements on Scripture ever written. For the sake of this book, I want to highlight a few of its teachings. First, the Scripture is sufficient as that which reveals "all things necessary for [God's] own glory, man's salvation, faith and life" (1.6). Second, the Scripture is "most necessary," or essential, in written form, since the "former ways of God's revealing his will unto his people [have] ceased" (1.1). Third, the Scripture is the authoritative rule over faith and life and the "supreme judge" in all theological "controversies" (1.10). Such authority depends not on man or the church "but wholly upon God (who is truth itself) the author thereof: and therefore it is to be received, because it is the Word of God" (1.4). In summary, as we unpack these five pillars, we could say this: the word of God alone is sufficient to set forth these teachings unto life, is essential for such teachings, and alone gives them their authority in our lives.

As we examine these five pillars in detail, we begin with the *Trinity-oriented life* unto God. While Jesus is the focal point of our faith and life, we need to grasp the triunity of the Godhead to understand Christ in his person and work. We then consider such a *Christ-focused life*, one that cannot be sustained unless it is simultaneously a *Spirit-energized life*. We turn to reflect on the bride of Christ, the church, and the obligation for a *church-inhabited life* if indeed we do belong to him. Finally, we look at a *heaven-anticipated life* with the hope of our future resurrected existence in the presence of Christ forever, though there is also an eternal punishment for those who find themselves outside Christ at death.

Summarizing the Christian faith in this way, I believe we have before us the basic building blocks for the Christian faith and thus for living for God. The building blocks can help, then, with the rest of the edifice, which has many layers and views from which to understand the truths that God has revealed to us, many of which lie outside the scope of this book but are important nonetheless.

PART 1

THE
TRINITY-ORIENTED
LIFE

1

The Triune God

If you are a Christian, you must love those who belong to Christ (John 13:35; 1 John 3:14). But do you love those who fought for the truth over the course of church history so that you could proclaim, know, and worship God in a clearer way based on the psychological, spiritual, and intellectual battles they fought? Many Christians have loved the doctrine of the Trinity; they have sometimes put their lives at risk for this doctrine. Shall we not love it both for God's sake and for the sake of all those who have offered their own blood, sweat, and tears for the cause of truth? I think we have a duty to God and our brothers and sisters in the Lord to love studying our triune God so that we may commune with each of the persons in the Godhead. We cannot commune with a God we do not know.

Christianity cannot exist or thrive without a robust understanding of the triune God. The principal distinguishing features of the Christian religion are its most glorious mysteries, namely, (1) the incarnation of the Son of God and (2) the triunity of God as one (essence) and yet three (persons). Whatever groans one may utter when studying the Trinity, such do not compare to the joys of knowing God as he truly is.

Many theologians and conference speakers decry the apparent lack of desire among Christians to learn more about our great God. There may exist no statistics to back up such a claim, but it certainly leaves us asking an important question about a crucial truth. Does the Trinity occupy a prominent place in our thinking or even in our meditation on God? Does the church adequately instruct the flock in the knowledge of the Father, Son, and Holy Spirit?

One God, Three Persons

The great distinctive of the Christian faith is the belief in the one, true, and living God (Deut. 6:4; 32:39; Isa. 44:8) in three distinct persons: the Father, the Son, and the Holy Spirit. Speaking of the one God, the Westminster Larger Catechism (q. 9) claims, "There be three persons in the Godhead, the Father, the Son, and the Holy [Spirit]; and these three are one true, eternal God, the same in substance, equal in power and glory; although distinguished by their personal properties" (e.g., Matt. 28:19; John 1:1; 10:30; Acts 5:3–4; 2 Cor. 13:14). In short, the doctrine of the Trinity implies unity in diversity.

Our monotheism must be regarded as Christian monotheism. We are neither polytheists, dismantling the Trinity with separated (not just distinct) gods, nor Monarchians, collapsing the Trinity into a single being with indistinguishable persons.[1] To be sure, we are limited in terms of how much we can discuss the Trinity, and saying more than God has revealed leads us astray and possibly into heresy. At the same time, denying this distinctive is done to the peril of our very soul. Someone, we do not know who, and not Augustine as some claim, has said,

"Try to explain the Trinity, and you will lose your mind; try to deny it, and you will lose your soul."[2] We may have trouble fully explaining what God has revealed concerning his triunity, but we must not deny that he is the triune God.

This much we must affirm: The Father is God (Rom. 7:25), the Son is God (Acts 20:28; Titus 2:13), and the Holy Spirit is God (Ps. 95:3, 8, 9, compared with Heb. 3; Acts 5:3–4; 1 Cor. 3:16–17). Yet there is one God. Within the Godhead, they remain distinct persons, as the Father is neither the Son nor the Spirit, and the Son is neither the Father nor the Spirit, and the Spirit is neither the Father nor the Son (e.g., Matt. 3:16–17).

This reality, that God is both one (essence) and three (persons), shapes everything about the Christian religion. It is a truth that all Christians have agreed on and will continue to agree on both now and forever. It is a truth that will occupy our heart, soul, mind, and strength in glory. The Nicene Creed (325; rev. 381) and the Apostles' Creed (ca. second–fourth centuries), two of the great truly ecumenical creeds of the Christian faith, both affirm the doctrine of the Trinity. But no early creed states so forcefully and clearly the central place the Christian faith gives to the doctrine of the Trinity like the Athanasian Creed (ca. fifth–seventh centuries). Notice how the first few sentences describe the truth of the Trinity:

> Whosoever will be saved, before all things it is necessary that he hold the catholic faith. Which faith unless every one do keep whole and undefiled, without doubt he shall perish everlastingly. And the catholic faith is this: that we worship one God in Trinity, and Trinity in Unity; neither confounding the Persons, nor dividing the Essence. For there is one Person of the Father; another of the Son; and another of the Holy Ghost. But the Godhead of the Father, of the Son, and

of the Holy Ghost, is all one; the Glory equal, the Majesty coeternal. Such as the Father is; such is the Son; and such is the Holy Ghost.[3]

Mere Christianity, basic Christianity, core Christianity, or whatever one wishes to call the foundational Christian faith is, at bottom, Trinitarian Christianity. The catholic faith, to which we belong, insists that we hold to this stunning truth that God is both three and one. So we believe in one God who subsists (exists) in three persons, all of whom share in the same single, undivided essence.[4] The three persons enjoy an interpenetration and yet remain perfectly together and eternally delight in themselves, owing to their infinite perfections. They exist in supreme and independent communion with each other as they co-indwell and co-inhere as three persons sharing the same undivided, infinitely pure essence. Theologians have historically used the terms *circumincession* (Latin-derived) or *perichoresis* (Greek-derived) to denote this intimate relationship among the persons of the Trinity.

If God were simply one person, he would have nobody but himself to love. If God were two persons, the love between them would not be shared with anyone else. But the glory of the Trinity is this: the love between the Father and the Son is also shared through the bond of the Spirit. "God is love" (1 John 4:8), but the love that characterizes God is a shared love between three persons.

The Triune God's Order and Works[5]

Because God is three persons, his self-love, which is infinitely and eternally delightful, is by nature "giving." God did not need to create the world, since he is in need of nothing outside himself, being eternally and infinitely independent. Still, he decided to create the world and perform outward acts that are consistent with the perfections of his nature.

The pioneering work of Augustine on the Trinity led to a theological commonplace that the outward works of the Trinity are undivided. In the words of the great theologian,

> For according to the Catholic faith, the Trinity is proposed to our belief and believed—and even understood by a few saints and holy persons—as so inseparable that whatever action is performed by it must be thought to be performed at the same time by the Father and by the Son and by the Holy Spirit.[6]

All three persons jointly concur in every work; they agree and cooperate in the works done by any one of them. For example, who raised Christ? The emphasis in the New Testament is clearly on the Father but not at the expense of the other two persons (John 2:19; 10:17–18; Rom. 4:24; 8:11; Col. 2:12–13). Because all three persons concur in every work, the Father, Son, and Holy Spirit are all said to have raised Christ from the dead.

With that in mind, while the outward works of the Trinity belong as much to one person as to the other two persons, certain (internal) works among the persons differ: the Father begets, the Son is begotten of the Father, and the Holy Spirit proceeds from the Father and the Son. Often the Father has been referred to as the "fountain of the deity," as he is the begetter, not the begotten.

As such, the persons have different subsistences, and therefore the works of each person follow and resemble their distinct existences. The Father, as the fountain of the deity, "begins" the work; the Son carries on the work; and the Holy Spirit, who proceeds from the Father and the Son, executes and consummates the works of the Father and the Son (1 Cor. 8:6). Consider Paul's opening Trinitarian emphasis in his letter to the Ephesians: the Father chooses us in the Son, "before the foundation of the world" (1:4); God the Father predestines through (and in) Jesus (1:4–5), in whom "we have redemption through his blood" (1:7); and the Holy Spirit perfects and consummates the works of the Father and the Son (1:13–14). Thus the outward works of God, while undivided, can be attributed particularly to one of the three persons.

While all three persons are coequal and coeternal, the Father is first in order, the Son is second in order, and the Spirit is third in order. Since the Spirit is last in order, he proceeds from the Father and the Son. He is the bond of the Trinity (i.e., between the Father and the Son), who proceeds by way of love. Just as the Spirit unites the Father and the Son, so the Spirit has the peculiar eminency of uniting sinners, saved by Christ's work, to Christ and thus also to the Father.

The Revealer of God

God does not hide his triunity from his people. As a personal God who shares of himself, he forces us to think of both his oneness and his threeness. Especially as the New Testament unfolds the further mystery of the Trinity, we ought to become enraptured by the Trinity, just as Gregory of Nazianzus was in his reflection on the oneness and threeness of God:

> No sooner do I conceive of the one than I am illumined by the splendour of the three; no sooner do I distinguish them than I am carried back to the one. When I think of any one of the three I think of him as the whole, and my eyes are filled, and the greater part of what I am thinking escapes me.

I cannot grasp the greatness of that one so as to attribute a greater greatness to the rest. When I contemplate the three together, I see but one torch, and cannot divide or measure out the undivided light.[7]

The principal manner in which God reveals himself as triune is through the life and prophetical ministry of his Son. The Son reveals the Father: "All things have been handed over to me by my Father, and no one knows who the Son is except the Father, or who the Father is except the Son and anyone to whom the Son chooses to reveal him" (Luke 10:22). The Son also reveals the Spirit, particularly in the Upper Room Discourse in John 14–16. For example, Christ speaks of the principal work of the Spirit in this way: "He [the Spirit] will glorify me, for he will take what is mine and declare it to you" (John 16:14).

Our Lord is not shy with his disciples about who he is, how he reveals the Father, and what the Spirit will do when he comes as the revealer of the Son. Thus we might say that God's interest in revealing himself to us is brought about by the ministry of the Lord Jesus Christ. The agent of revelation is actually Christ.

The mediator of God's saving knowledge to us comes in the Son. Christ is the beam of light[8] by which God's glories, perfections, and purposes are revealed to his people. The intimate knowledge the Son had of the Father before his incarnation is one that is shared. The Son comes into the world for many reasons, not just one. But perhaps most significantly, his coming is to make God known: "No one has ever seen God; the only God, who is at the Father's side, he has made him known" (John 1:18). Not only God's triunity but also his invisible attributes are revealed most clearly in the person and work of the Son, who is the stage on which the attributes come into full view.

Practical Trinitarianism

The foundational Christian faith necessitates our embrace of the doctrine of the Trinity but not necessarily in all its details and complexities. The great Princeton theologian Charles Hodge offers what might be sort of the lowest bar for the professing Christian concerning one's affirmation of the Trinity, by way of an

> unconscious or unformed faith, even of those of God's people who are unable to understand the term by which it is expressed. They all believe in God, the Creator and Preserver. . . . They . . . believe in a divine Redeemer and a divine Sanctifier. They have, as it were, the factors of the doctrine of the Trinity in their own religious convictions.[9]

The expectations of the Athanasian Creed above certainly seem to rise higher than the expectations of Hodge living in the nineteenth century—and one might say our expectations have dropped even lower well over one hundred years on. One could, I suppose, on Hodge's account have such a basic understanding of the Trinity to be practically a modalist (though not a philosophically committed modalist), that is, to hold that God—as one person—takes on the roles of Preserver, Redeemer, and Sanctifier, but I think most Christians would happily confess that the Father, as Creator and Preserver, sends the Son, as Redeemer. Additionally, the Spirit, as Sanctifier, is sent by the Father and the Son. In sum, Christians, educated in God's holy word, are privileged to know that there are three divine persons, who all play crucial roles in their lives and their salvation.

Yet in discoursing on the Trinity and other such wondrous doctrines, the "prince of the Puritans," John Owen, makes the observation that the Trinity, for example, when first proposed to God's people, "startles" us, since the truths of the Trinity are "too great and too excellent" for us to take in. But over time, with instruction, our nature "yields" and submits to that which God reveals. Owen asks, "What is there, in the whole book of God, that nature at first sight does more recoil at, than the doctrine of the Trinity? How many do yet stumble and fall at it!"[10] He then argues that unless we embrace the doctrine of the Trinity, when it is proposed and explained to us, "all other things [e.g., communion with God] wherein it has to do with God will not be of value to the soul." Owen adds, "Take away, then, the doctrine of the Trinity, and . . . the foundation of all fruits of love and goodness is lost to the soul."[11]

What Owen implies is that the doctrine of the Trinity may be misunderstood or unknown to a new Christian who is growing in and responding to the glorious teaching of Scripture on the Trinity. Once fleshed out to the understanding of the maturing believer, it must be embraced. It is one thing to lack understanding of the doctrine and quite another to deny it.

"Mere Trinitarianism," as in a minimalist affirmation, may indeed look a lot like what Hodge speaks of—and there is much good even in such a basic affirmation. But basic Trinitarianism brings the soul much further, to the point where Christian worship (public and private) and life (corporate and individual) become more and more Trinity oriented. Christianity demands the affirmation that God is one essence but also three coequal persons. But it is certainly more: the foundation of all our communion, delight, hope, and thanksgiving are dependent on our knowledge of the triune God and the ways in which he relates to us as distinct persons—Father, Son, and Holy Spirit.

2

Communion with the Triune God

As human beings, we relate to people constantly, whether on a one-to-one level or in a group setting. Our identity, even as individuals, is wrapped up in our relationships with others. There's something good about this insofar as we are made in God's image as relational beings. If one looks at the life of Jesus, one can't help but notice what an intensely relational person he was. He loved to communicate with people. We should take note of this.

In the beginning, Adam was made to relate to (God) his Father. It was natural for Adam to seek and know God, to enjoy him as his highest end. This was always God's intention for humanity, namely, that they should be brought to God—something Christ's death accomplished (1 Pet. 3:18).

One of the many glories of the Christian life is the reality that God is relational and that (despite our sin) he continues to relate to us by way of grace. He is not a distant deity, but he actually relates to his people by communing with them in a way appropriate to his triunity. It's common to hear evangelicals speaking of "a personal relationship with Jesus Christ." Whatever individual Christians may mean by this in their particular usage, the phrase is not without merit. But a foundational Christian faith for living to God demands that such a statement be explained in a manner that does justice to God's triunity as well as to the corporate aspects of "relational" theology.

Corporate Communion[1]

The three persons of the Godhead are all distinct, living, divine, and intelligent persons. They not only act inwardly toward one another, but they also act outwardly in a special manner toward those on whom they have set their love. I am tempted, following much of North American Christian piety, to focus first on the relation of the individual believer to the triune God in their daily lives, but Christianity, as I understand it, follows the emphases of the Scriptures in connection with a wise dependence on what has been handed down to the church by her teachers (e.g., theologians and pastors). The highest point of our Christian lives is corporate worship.

The triune God created us to worship him, which is his prerogative as God (Ps. 95:6; Rev. 4:11; 14:7). When we worship God, we are at our best. Likewise, when we worship anything else, we are at our worst. The scriptural reference to "worship" toward God carries with it a sense of falling or bowing down to God. With our entire being, individually and corporately, we worship with all our mind, heart, soul, and strength. In response to what the triune God has revealed of himself, we ought to offer up ourselves as "living sacrifice[s]," as something "acceptable to God," and as our "spiritual worship" (Rom. 12:1) by offering ourselves completely.

As implied above, worship of God involves the whole person (Deut. 6:4–6). We apply our hearts and minds to God's glory; to his many attributes, such as holiness, majesty, and power (1 Chron. 16:29; Ps. 29:1–4); and to his triunity (Matt. 28:18–20). Our wills submit to God's majesty and power, our hearts embrace his goodness, and we enter into communion with the Father, Son, and Holy Spirit.

As creatures, we are to worship God, but as sinful creatures, we are unable to fulfill this obligation apart from Jesus Christ. Sin has perverted our worship and caused us to pursue the created rather than the Creator (Rom. 1:20–25). We can be restored only through the saving work of Christ. Thus, the prayer of the psalmist is for God's "way" and "saving power" to be known "among all nations" (Ps. 67:2). Why? That "all the peoples" would "praise" him (Ps. 67:5). From such a prayer comes our motivation to bring the gospel to others—that they may worship our triune God. As John Piper rightly attests, "Missions exists because worship doesn't."[2] Redemption in Christ restores our relationship with God, and such leads to our communion with and worship of him. Christ, as mediator, bridges the gap between God's holiness and our sin (1 Tim. 2:5), establishing a covenant relationship between us.

All knowledge of God, and so all worship of him, is rooted in a divine covenant (Pss. 25:14; 50:14–16). God begins this relationship, and we respond. He comes in love, and we respond in love; he comes in glory, and we respond in reverence (Heb. 12:28). Not only did the Father send Christ into the world to bridge the gap between fallen man and a thrice-holy God, but also, in the outworking of redemption, the Father and the Son sent the Holy Spirit to enable us to worship in the Spirit, not purely in our own might. Hence our worship is Spirit energized.

The centrality of Christ's mediation in the context of the covenant is a gift to the church, for we pray in his name, and in the new covenant, priests are no longer necessary (Heb. 8–9). While worship can take an individualistic form, the corporate aspect of worship dominates the pages of Scripture, particularly in the new covenant, where worship is almost exclusively so. This reflects the growing maturity of the church (that is, Christ's body) and God's intention to have a treasured people for himself (Ex. 19:5–6; 1 Pet. 2:9). The goal of evangelism is to be involved in gathering such a people from all nations to worship the Father, Son, and Spirit (Ps. 67; Isa. 2:2–4; Matt. 28:18–20).

On the Lord's Day, the corporate nature of worship reaches its zenith. Using the body analogy, Paul argues against a sort of "communism," in which each person has the same function or role in worship. On the contrary, each member is a particular part of the body and therefore performs a different function. True, all Christians are part of the royal priesthood (1 Pet. 2:9), but we minister differently according to the gifting of the Holy Spirit (1 Cor. 12). Our worship consists not only of singing but also of listening, praying, and Communion. Worship responds to God's acts and revelation in the Scriptures. For these reasons, worship must be in the power of the Spirit and according to truth (John 4:24).

Worship is transformative: we become like what we worship (Ps. 115:8). For Christians, that means that as we now, by faith, in the power of the Spirit, behold the glory of God in the face of Jesus Christ, we are being transformed into his likeness (2 Cor. 3:18; 4:6). Moreover, worship transcends time and place: though we are on earth, it is performed in heaven (Heb. 12:22–24).

Worship is giving glory to God for his worth in the name of Jesus by the power of the Holy Spirit according to truth. We praise God, who gave to the church both his Son and the Spirit, who, besides himself, was the best he had to give. In response to Christ's sacrifice, we become living sacrifices as we behold the glory of God in the face of Jesus Christ, who is the new temple and draws all nations to himself (Isa. 2:2–3). This is our delight as Christians.

Communion with God

Communion, in general, involves a mutual relationship where, hopefully, good things are communicated. The closer the union between those in communion, the better the communion should be (e.g., the Trinity, marriage). In Christian worship the primary emphasis should be on what God can do for us and in us, not principally on what we can do for God. God calls us to worship him; he is the initiator in all things. He communicates good things to us so that we may, in return, offer that which is pleasing and acceptable in his sight, namely, our love, trust, and obedience (see John 14:23; 1 Cor. 1:9; 12:4–6; 2 Cor. 13:14; 1 John 1:3; 1:7; Rev. 3:4).

In *On Christian Doctrine*, Augustine writes, "The true objects of enjoyment, then, are the Father and the Son and the Holy Spirit, who are at the same time the Trinity, one Being, supreme above all, and common to all who enjoy Him."[3] The aim of communion is enjoyment. The best enjoyments are received and given in love. As J. I. Packer has said, "Communion with God is a relationship in which Christians receive love from, and respond in love to, all three persons of the Trinity."[4]

Corporate Christian worship should foster both a desire to commune with the triune God and the knowledge of how to do so. We do not learn to commune with God privately and then go to church to listen, sing, and pray. We go to church to worship the triune God, and to the extent that corporate worship fails to bring home to God's people his triunity and why we should love each person in the Godhead, such worship has failed in the final analysis. It has failed because it is not cultivating, as it must, the personal communion we must enjoy with each person.

Thomas Goodwin, a great Puritan writer, speaks of the communion believers are to enjoy with each person of the Trinity:

> Sometimes a man's communion and converse is with the one, sometimes with the other; sometimes with the Father, then with the Son, and then with the Holy Ghost; sometimes his heart is drawn out to consider the Father's love in choosing, and then the love of Christ in redeeming, and so again the love of the Holy Ghost, that searches the deep things of God, and reveals them to us, and takes all the pains with us; and so a man goes from one witness to another distinctly. . . . We should never be satisfied till all three persons lie level in us, and all make their abode with us, and we sit as it were in the midst of them, while they all manifest their love unto us.[5]

If at the heart of our Christian faith we are not, both corporately and privately, enjoying the love of the triune God toward us, then we are living a life quite unlike what God intends for those who love him and are loved by him. We all need to be confronted a great deal more with our daily response to the triune God than we are in what currently passes for much Christian spirituality.

Communion with the Father

When we think of the Father, two dominant thoughts ought to be uppermost in our minds: (1) that we have been reconciled to the Father (Rom. 5:11; 2 Cor. 5:17–19) and (2) that this reconciliation to him is a result of his freely given love that has been poured into our hearts through the Spirit. Consider these passages:

> Anyone who does not love does not know God, because God is love. In this the love of God was made manifest among us, that God sent his only Son into the world, so that we might live through him. (1 John 4:8–9)

> The grace of the Lord Jesus Christ and the love of God and the fellowship of the Holy Spirit be with you all. (2 Cor. 13:14)

> In that day you will ask in my name, and I do not say to you that I will ask the Father on your behalf; for the Father himself loves you, because you have loved me and have believed that I came from God. (John 16:26–27)

> And hope does not put us to shame, because God's love has been poured into our hearts through the Holy Spirit who has been given to us. (Rom. 5:5)

Why did God choose to save us? The Father loved us for the sake of his Son. In eternity, God freely fixed his love on us in Christ. Because God is unchangeable, his love to us in Christ is unchangeable. The best answer I can come up with for why God loved us is this: he loves his Son and aims to glorify him. Saving us is one way in which the Father glorifies the Son (John 17:10). So we can do a little better than saying God loves us because he loves us: we can focus on his love for us for the sake of his Son.

Love is not always easy to define, even when Paul defines it as gloriously as he does in 1 Corinthians 13. Love from God the Father to us and back to him includes a love of union, satisfaction, and goodwill. These are the parts of the highest form of love. The love of union means that the Father brings us to himself through our union with the Son (Isa. 54:5–8; 2 Cor. 5:17–21). But God not only reconciles us to himself, he also has a love of satisfaction toward us: he loves us and delights in us for the good he sees in us (Ps. 149:4; Gal. 5:22). We likewise delight in him for the infinite good that is in him (Pss. 104–106). Finally, God has a love of goodwill toward us; he grants us blessings from above (Ps. 85:12; 1 Cor. 4:7; James 1:17). We, in return, devote ourselves to God, giving him our best: worship. We acknowledge his love toward us and respond in love to our Father, who did not spare his own Son, so that we may be spared (Rom. 8:32).

Christian worship, both in the company of the upright and in private, must love the love of the Father toward us. The basic Christian faith demands that all God's people are acquainted, for their good, with the love their heavenly Father has for them and the subsequent enjoyment we possess in loving back such a God. This was indeed how the Son communed with his Father on earth: "But I do as the Father has commanded me, so that the world may know that I love the Father" (John 14:31). He loved his Father because his Father loved him: "This is my beloved Son, with whom I am well pleased" (Matt. 3:17). Hence, both Christ and believers, when thinking about the Father, must think of him as filled with love toward his children, for he is the great fountain and spring of love toward his Son and his Son's bride.

Communion with the Son

In the classic Trinitarian benediction in 2 Corinthians 13:14, Paul says, "The grace of the Lord Jesus Christ and the love of God and the fellowship of the Holy Spirit be with you all." Jesus is the one who "became flesh," possessing glory, "glory as of the only Son from the Father, full of grace and truth" (John 1:14). From Christ's glory as the God-man, we have received "grace upon grace" (John 1:16).

It is not as though we do not commune with Christ in love, but rather, this love is specified by the grace of his person as the God-man and the work he did for us poor, miserable sinners. We focus distinctly on these aspects since Christ alone gave up his life for us in an act of love that revealed his grace toward us. Christ does not add to the Father's love for us, but he does draw it out through grace.

Again, like our communion with the Father, the manner in which we commune in grace with Christ is both corporate and personal. In the corporate setting, not only is Christ the content of the Bible, so that every sermon should lead to him and exalt him, but Christ is presented to God's people in the sacraments of baptism and the Lord's Supper.

In the context of corporate worship, God's people are privileged to have "Jesus Christ . . . publicly portrayed as crucified" (Gal. 3:1). There's a glorious objectivity in communion with Christ that takes place on the Lord's Day. Christ gifts to the church ministers and teachers who are (supposed to be) equipped to present the glories of the glorious one to those who, by beholding his glory, will be changed into his image from one degree to another (2 Cor. 3:18).

To the degree that Christ's person and work are clearly proclaimed, the person of the Father and the person of the Spirit come into clearer view. What is the love of the Father if it is divorced from the gift of his Son? What is the work of the Spirit if it is does not come in the name of Christ? Communion with Christ will inevitably lead to communion with the Father and the Spirit. After all, since God is one, this is the only true test of whether one's communion with a distinct person in the Godhead is real: Does it lead to a greater knowledge of and love for all three persons?

Ultimately, however grand and beautiful the truth of the Father's love and the Son's grace toward us may be, it will profit us nothing if the Spirit does not enable us to enjoy these benefits by his energized work in us.

Communion with the Spirit

Jesus promised to his distressed disciples a "Counselor" (i.e., the Paraclete), as in a legal counselor (John 16:7–11 CSB).[6] But the Spirit's work, as the various English translations show, is to comfort God's people so that he strengthens and helps them (thus "Helper," ESV). The coming of the Spirit, in the name of Jesus (Rom. 8:9), brings in a new age, so to speak (Isa. 11:1–10; 32:14–18; 42:1–4; 44:1–5; Ezek. 11:17–20; 36:24–27; 37:1–14; Joel 2:28–32). In light of the resurrection and ascension of Jesus, who is now seated at the right hand of God the Father, the Spirit ministers to Christ's bride by powerfully indwelling the people of God.

Because God is one, to have the Spirit dwelling in us, we necessarily have the Father and the Son dwelling in our body-souls. This much is clear from the Upper Room Discourse in John 14. Divine presence in a believer includes the Spirit (John 14:15–17), the Son (John 14:18–21), and the Father (John 14:22–24).

With this in mind, believers put their trust in the promises of the comfort of the Spirit and pray for the ongoing work and influence of the Holy Spirit in their lives (Luke 11:13; John 7:37–39; Gal. 3:2, 14). We have, as those who possess the Spirit, a responsibility to continually seek the Spirit. Such seeking of the

Spirit will naturally lead us to a greater awareness of the Father's love and Christ's grace. In other words, our fellowship with God depends on the Spirit: "The fellowship of the Holy Spirit be with you all" (2 Cor. 13:14).

The Spirit communes with each believer in numerous ways:

1. He glorifies Christ.
2. He pours out the love of God into our hearts.
3. He witnesses to the believer that he or she is a child of God.
4. He seals faith in the Christian.
5. He assures the believer of salvation.
6. He becomes to the Christian the Spirit of supplication.[7]

Not to belabor the point, but the various works of the Spirit toward believers occur primarily in the context of the gathered church. Where else may one so vividly experience the work of the Spirit than in the context where true worship is taking place among many who are gathered in the name of Christ? By all means, take every opportunity to pray for the powerful indwelling of the Spirit in your life, but never forget that the Spirit works in conjunction with the word of God and that his chief aim is to glorify Christ. Thus, where that happens, there the Spirit will be.

The Sum of the Matter

If Christian experience is understood first as corporate and second as personal, then we are to commune with the persons of the Trinity in both ways. Much of our corporate worship lacks a Trinitarian emphasis, whether, for example, in the order of worship or in the content of the public prayers. With this in mind, one should not be surprised if the Trinity does not find its way into our meditations on and prayers toward God.

As we commune with the three persons in public and in private, the doctrine of the Trinity will be strengthened in our souls. All the excellent truths of the Christian faith are practical truths meant to enrich our needy souls that depend on power from on high. As John Owen says,

> What is so high, glorious, and mysterious as the doctrine of the ever-blessed Trinity? Some wise men have thought meet to keep it veiled from ordinary Christians, and some have delivered it in such terms as that they can understand nothing by them. But take a believer who has tasted how gracious the Lord is, in the eternal love of the Father, the great undertaking of the Son in the work of mediation and redemption, with the almighty work of the Spirit creating grace and comfort in the soul; and has had an experience of the love, holiness, and power of God in them all; and he will with more firm confidence adhere to this mysterious truth, being led into it and confirmed in it by some few plain testimonies of the word, than a thousand disputers shall do who only have a notion of it in their minds.[8]

The only way to truly experience God is to experience the one true God in his threeness as Father, Son, and Holy Spirit. As the apostle Paul says, "For through [Christ] we . . . have access in one Spirit to the Father" (Eph. 2:18). Christ reveals the Trinity to us for our good and for God's glory.

3

The Majestic Triune God

The Scottish philosopher and mathematician Dugald Steward (1753–1828) noted, "Every man has some peculiar train of thought which he falls back upon when he is alone. This, to a great degree, moulds the man."[1] As Christians, what do we think about when we are alone? Charles Spurgeon said, "Good thoughts are blessed guests, and should be heartily welcomed, well fed, and much sought after. Like rose leaves, they give out a sweet smell if laid up in the jar of memory."[2] I propose to you: meditate on and come to an increasing knowledge of the triune God's attributes. It will do you much good.

What do great thoughts about the three persons of the Trinity have to do with our Christian life? How should we think about the greatness of God in worship, and whose responsibility is it to foster such meditations and praises? Here, I say, the clergy—many of whom have been trained at seminary—need to take responsibility for shaping the types of thoughts those in their flock have about God. In some cases, the people of God are (rightly) pushed intellectually and spiritually in a healthy way; in other cases, many remain in third grade, happy with the basics but unaware of what they are missing out on.

The Father, Son, and Holy Spirit all share something in common without even the smallest hint of difference. To say that of three persons is impossible, unless those three persons share the same singular, undivided divine essence. Such is the case with our triune God.

God Is Great

Christians need to have great thoughts of God because God is great:

> For the LORD is a great God,
>   and a great King above all gods. (Ps. 95:3)

But many Christians lack great thoughts of God because the worship service they attend each week does not foster great thoughts of God. How does your worship service enable you to be in awe of God (Heb. 12:28)?

Many in the present-day church sing and pray about God but not always in very specific ways. Some evangelical churches ignore the rich heritage of psalms and hymns that express in substance the majesty and worth of the triune God. Instead, like one taking up a Styrofoam cup in the place of a crystal goblet, they opt for theologically simplistic, repetitive songs that fail to move beyond a few of God's essential attributes. I am not here condemning all usage of contemporary songs in worship—since many are excellent—but advocating care in what we communicate of God to our people, so that believers may grow deeper in knowing and relating with the triune God. That's why I'm concerned that watered-down music contributes to watered-down Christianity.

Saying God is great or good is one thing, but even a Muslim or a (religious) Jew can do that. Great hymns tell great stories about God, and no one—especially a Jew or Muslim—can possibly sing "Come, Thou Almighty King" or "Holy, Holy, Holy" without a profound sense of the greatness of the *triune* God. "And Can It Be?," by Charles Wesley, is a powerful exposition of Christ's love for sinners; it requires of us such mind-stretching and soul-bursting theology when we affirm that our God (i.e., the Son) has died for us ("That thou, my God, shouldst die for me").

Returning to the Psalms and their place in our thoughts about God, to sing Psalm 93:1–5 is to audibly, from our hearts, say things about our God that he completely agrees with:

> The LORD reigns; he is robed in majesty;
>> the LORD is robed; he has put on strength as his belt.
> Yes, the world is established; it shall never be moved.
> Your throne is established from of old;
>> you are from everlasting.
>
> The floods have lifted up, O LORD,
>> the floods have lifted up their voice;
>> the floods lift up their roaring.
> Mightier than the thunders of many waters,
>> mightier than the waves of the sea,
>> the LORD on high is mighty!
>
> Your decrees are very trustworthy;
>> holiness befits your house,
> O LORD, forevermore.

God commands us to praise his "great and awesome name" (Ps. 99:3). As we exalt the triune God, we worship him at his footstool (Ps. 99:5). This is our only fitting response to who

God is and to what he has done for us. As Augustine says in the opening lines of *The Confessions*, "We humans . . . long to praise you. . . . You stir us so that praising you may bring us joy, because you have made us and drawn us to yourself, and our heart is unquiet until it rests in you."[3]

Our souls can be satisfied only by a true knowledge of the triune God. We have a feast of riches offered to us in his word, but we are like a person who sits down at the world-famous Eleven Madison Park restaurant with the opportunity to enjoy an eleven-course retrospective tasting menu but is content with the first two courses and goes home, picking up a Big Mac on the way. Such a scenario would be tragic, but it is not nearly as much so as our willful refusal to learn about God in ways that remain consistent with the total scope of his revelation to us.

Knowing God

God is a spirit. The triune God is infinite, eternal, and unchangeable; he is wisdom, justice, goodness, and truth. He is love, but he is infinitely, eternally, and powerfully loving. His incomprehensibility means that God is simply too awesome for us to gaze on and (ever) fully know. His presence, if revealed to us in its supreme glory, would consume us in an instant. Speaking to Moses, God said, "You cannot see my face, for man shall not see me and live" (Ex. 33:20). Hence God had to reveal himself to Moses, ultimately, in the person of Christ on the Mount of Transfiguration (i.e., Mount Hermon) for Moses to see his glory and live (Matt. 17:3).

God condescends to our weaknesses and reveals himself in such a way that we are, ordinarily speaking, not consumed (John 1:14)—though some have not always fared so well (Ex. 15:7–10). Now it must be said, and most emphatically, that whatever attribute is ascribed to the Father, the same must be said about the Son and the Spirit when discussing the divine attributes. God is one; the Father cannot be omnipotent (all powerful) in a manner that is distinct or superior to the other two persons; otherwise, we may become (heretical) Arians— confessing Christ as somehow less than fully God. The Father is almighty, the Son is almighty, and the Spirit is almighty. But there is only one essence, which means that these are not three "Almighties" but that the three persons are all Almighty God.

Principally, God has revealed himself to us through his word. The Lord Jesus Christ, who is also called the Word (John 1:1), is the content of God's revelation to us. The Scriptures come from the lips of Christ, mediated through human beings, and they lead us back to Christ, who is the mediator between man and God. As John Calvin says in his commentary on Acts 7:30, "Let us, first of all, set down this for a surety, that there was never since the beginning any communication between God and men, save only by Christ."[4] In our response to the words of Christ, the Spirit makes it possible for our faith to return to God with praise, understanding, and worship that pleases him.

Without Christ's mediation between God and man, we would be in a precarious position indeed. How could we come to a true knowledge of God apart from Christ? The truth is, our knowledge of God, even by seeing his invisible attributes displayed in creation, would ultimately be mixed with so much falsehood that we would all be walking idolaters on an earth that testifies plainly to the glory of God. As a blind man describes the painting in the Sistine Chapel, so a sinful human being, apart from revelation, describes God.

Thus, Christ gives us the clearest picture of God; he is, after all, the visible image of the invisible God (Col. 1:15). To know

Christ is to know who God is toward us—and that is to know who God is. If God is "holy, holy, holy," then his holiness revealed toward us is that of Christ (Isa. 6:1–3; John 12:41). God cannot reveal his infinite holiness toward us apart from the mediation of Christ; otherwise, we would be destroyed and thrown into outer darkness.

God's Attributes

God is a most pure spirit who is simple. God is one essence, so when we speak of his attributes in the plural, we are allowing for a manner of speaking that is technically incorrect since God is not the sum of various parts. As such, his goodness is his power is his eternity is his unchangeability is his wisdom is his knowledge and so on. This means, therefore, that God's attributes are not only infinite but also perfectly consistent with each other. As the infinite one, God has no limit to his perfections. His power, for example, is intensively and qualitatively infinite. Without bounds or limits or degrees, God is. God knows infinitely; he is a sphere whose center is everywhere and circumference nowhere.[5]

God's eternity is a mind-boggling concept. We are creatures of time, with successions of moments. But God has no beginning, middle, or end; rather, he is timeless and therefore unchangeable (yet not static), possessing an eternal present, whereby he knows all that can be known. It is more proper to say that time began with the creature than that the creature began with time. God's eternity means he is unchangeable (James 1:17). He is what he always was and will be, without any change whatsoever. If God is eternal, which speaks about the duration of his state, then immutability is the state itself. God does not and cannot change (Ps. 102:26–27) because he is infinite and eternal. If one attribute is compromised, then every attribute is compromised.

Unlike us, God is independent. He is all-sufficient in himself, needing nothing outside himself. His self-sufficiency, which is eternal and infinite, means that he can provide enough gifts to his creatures without any injury or harm to himself. He can satisfy us to the greatest measure that creatures can possibly receive his goodness. The Father, Son, and Holy Spirit (eternally and unchangeably) satisfy each other in love. This reality is the basis for how the three persons can satisfy us for the rest of our eternal existence. God is life, fully and pervasively. Thus we derive our life—the good life—from the infinitely good, absolutely independent God.

God's power enables him to satisfy us out of his independence. God possesses an absolute power and an ordained power (Matt. 26:53–54; Mark 14:36). His absolute power refers to what God is able to do (e.g., create fifty billion worlds). God's ordained power refers to what he has chosen, out of his free will, to do: create a world for his Son, Jesus Christ, to be the heir of all things. God providentially accomplishes this because he is the sovereign Lord. These "powers" are not two distinct powers in God but a way to understand his omnipotence by way of application (i.e., ordained power) and nonapplication (i.e., absolute power). Nothing happens unless he has willed it to happen (Acts 17:26; Eph. 1:11). Christianity requires God's sovereign lordship over all things.

Much of our comfort in the Christian life arises out of the indisputable fact that God orders all things for his glory and our good. As the Westminster Confession of Faith states so succinctly,

> God from all eternity, did, by the most wise and holy counsel of his own will, freely, and unchangeably ordain whatsoever comes to pass; yet so, as thereby neither is God the author of

sin, nor is violence offered to the will of the creatures; nor is the liberty or contingency of second causes taken away, but rather established. (3.1)

We will never fully understand how it is that we possess freedom in our actions and yet that God is also free to order *all* things after the counsel of his will (Rom. 8:28; 11:33; Eph. 1:10). Nonetheless, we delight in the truth that we are free and yet fully in the providential care of our sovereign Lord, who does not leave things to chance.

Why is it that we struggle with grand thoughts about our triune God? As noted at the beginning of this chapter, our problem is obvious: much of our corporate worship, personal Bible reading, and preaching is terribly truncated. We are unfamiliar with the God of Job, we know few of the 150 psalms, and pastors rarely preach on verses and chapters in books like Isaiah or Ezekiel. We may not need to spend three years in Isaiah, but even three weeks might do our souls much good.

The Christian faith demands that we come to a place in our lives where God is the one beyond whom nothing better can be conceived. Not spouses or children or material possessions or food but God is that than which nothing greater can be loved and adored. Who he is and what he has done for his Son and for us demand our life, our souls, our all.

Praising God

If a Christian cannot praise God for who he is during this life, then one must wonder whether such a person has any desire to be in heaven in the life to come, where unceasing praise of God and the wholesome knowledge of his various attributes will take place. Praise does not have to be a boring endeavor, so long as we are equipped to speak of God in ways that are rich and vivid.

Consider Augustine's praise of God in his monumental work *The Confessions*:

> You are most high, excellent, most powerful, omnipotent, supremely merciful and supremely just, most hidden yet intimately present, infinitely beautiful and infinitely strong, steadfast yet elusive, unchanging yourself though you control the change in all things, never new, never old, renewing all things yet wearing down the proud though they know it not; ever active, ever at rest, gathering while knowing no need, supporting and filling and guarding, creating and nurturing and perfecting, seeking although you lack for nothing. You love without frenzy, you are jealous yet secure, you regret without sadness, you grow angry yet remain tranquil, you alter your works but never your plan; you take back what you find although you never lost it; you are never in need yet you rejoice in your gains. . . . After saying all that, what have we said, my God, my life, my holy sweetness? What does anyone who speaks of you really say?[6]

As Christians, we need to know that we cannot know God fully. And we can never speak adequately of all his perfections. But as Augustine also noted in his *Confessions*, "Woe to those who fail to speak of God."[7] His eternal existence, whereby he has no beginning and no end, should excite us. He will always love us because he never "began" to love us (i.e., he has always, as the eternal God, loved us).

We can never fully know the infinite God, which is his glory and, in another sense, also ours. That is good news for us, for who would like to worship a god who can be fully known? Such a god is devised only for us to control, not to humbly worship. We can know God truly because he reveals himself to us—in "baby language," so to speak—through his word. The word of God (the Scripture) testifies to the Word of God (the Son). So to know what God is like is to know Jesus, who is the perfect representation of God to our finite minds. Nothing gives us a clearer picture of God than the one who is the God-man. As we read of the great God of Job and Isaiah, we are reading of a God who also condescended in the most remarkable way to become flesh and assume to himself properties (e.g., hunger, thirst, weakness) that seem radically different from infinity, power, and blessedness (see 2 Cor. 13:4).

Christianity in its most basic expression begins with God because there is nowhere else to begin. Yet the Christian faith not only begins with God but also leads to him and continues in that continual searching out of his majestic glory. And whatever truth we acknowledge of God's majestic attributes, we acknowledge of the Father, Son, and Holy Spirit. Think about your God in his majesty but also of the Father, Son, and Holy Spirit. Each person possesses infinite power, glory, and might. Each possesses unlimited wisdom, knowledge, and blessedness. In Anselm of Canterbury's *Proslogium*, he offers a stirring exhortation to his readers that we desperately need today:

> Up now, slight man! Flee, for a little while, your occupations; hide yourself, for a time, from your disturbing thoughts. Cast aside, now, your burdensome cares, and put away your toilsome business. Yield room for some little time to God; and rest for a little time in him. Enter the inner chamber of your mind; shut out all thoughts except that of God, and such as can aid you in seeking him; close your door and seek him. Speak now, my whole heart! Speak now to God, saying, I seek your face; your face, Lord, will I seek (Ps. 27:8). And come now, O Lord my God, teach my heart where and how it may seek you, where and how it may find you.[8]

Praying to the Trinity

In light of Anselm's exhortation "Speak now to God," I want to close this chapter with some reflections on our prayers to God. Communion with our triune God implies the pursuit of a relationship with each of the persons of the Trinity. So let me ask, have you ever had a relationship with someone you never speak to? No, of course not! This being the case, have you ever noticed that you rarely hear anyone speaking directly to the triune God or to all three persons of the Trinity distinctly in prayer? I would make the case that it is entirely warranted and even advocated to pray to our triune God in general and to each of the persons specifically and that in so doing, we cultivate communion with the one God in three persons.

Indeed, Jesus prayed to the Father and taught us to do the same (e.g., Matt. 6:6, 9; John 17:1). Most prayers you hear are addressed to our "Father" and understandably so. Even with what I advocate about Trinitarian prayers, we can never go wrong by praying to the Father (Matt. 6:9) in the name of Jesus (John 16:23) and by way of the Spirit (Eph. 6:18; cf. Rom. 15:30). Still, we have warrant to go further in a Trinity-oriented approach to the Christian life.

Often, you will also hear people addressing God as "Lord," which is certainly fine, though we may be left wondering whether they are praying specifically to Jesus. Such prayers, of course, find warrant in Scripture, as with Stephen, who clearly cried out, "Lord Jesus, receive my spirit" (Acts 7:59), and with John, who exclaimed, "Come, Lord Jesus" (Rev. 22:20). That there exists no specific instruction to pray to Jesus should not concern us then. Did the disciples speak to the God-man on earth and so grow in their communion with him? Shall we speak to him in heaven and in the new heavens and earth and experience the same? Of course, to both questions. Then why should we not speak to him now?

Prayer to the Holy Spirit presents perhaps the greatest challenge. The Bible includes neither specific instructions for nor examples of praying to the Holy Spirit. We are only told to pray "in the Spirit" (e.g., Eph. 6:18). Sometimes when you hear or read people addressing this question, they call attention to such factors, without either expressly forbidding or openly encouraging prayers to the Holy Spirit, who is indeed the third person of the Trinity after all. In encouraging communion with the Holy Spirit, I wish to fully advocate prayers to him. Indeed, if he is God (Acts 5:3–4), our Comforter and Guide (John 14:26; 16:13), the one who utters up prayers on our behalf and helps us in our weakness (Rom. 8:26), and one with whom we are to pursue communion, then we ought to speak to him.

I would further contend that we are given explicit instructions for and examples of prayer to the Holy Spirit in the general instructions concerning prayer to God (Pss. 4:1; 17:6; 55:16; 57:2; 2 Cor. 13:7; James 1:5). We are to ask for the Spirit from the Father and the Son, but in asking for the filling of the Spirit, we certainly should be including the Spirit in our specific petition. If the God of Scripture is the triune God, we have full warrant to address him, and any of the three persons in the one God, as such. So when David attested in Psalm 17:6, "I call upon you, for you will answer me, O God; incline your ear to me; hear my words," he could just as well have said, "O triune God," or "O Holy Spirit." This is not exegetical gymnastics but simply, with Gregory of Nazianzus, being drawn to the three when reflecting on the one.

PART 2

THE CHRIST-FOCUSED LIFE

4

Person

John Campbell Shairp (1819–1885), a Scottish professor of poetry at Oxford, movingly wrote, "That image, or rather that Person, so human, yet so entirely divine, has a power to fill imagination, to arrest the affections, to deepen and purify the conscience, which nothing else in the world has."[1] Those who write about Jesus must do so in a way that does some justice to the glory of the person.

Of the three persons in the blessed Trinity, the Son was the one who assumed to himself a true human nature, consisting of both a body and a soul. The redemption of sinners is premised on this great fact, namely, that God the Son became a man and will forever remain, from the time of the incarnation, both fully God and fully man. Unless he assumed a true human nature, it would be impossible for him to save even one human.

Let me stress this point: we are never on the right track when we speak of salvation in terms of what Christ did for us without understanding who Christ is for us. The worth of his person exceeds the value of his work, since he eternally exists in all his perfections without needing to do a thing for our sakes. Hence the great Christian confession, before the Apostles' Creed or the Nicene Creed, that comes from the pen of the apostle Paul:

Great indeed, we confess, is the mystery of godliness:

> He was manifested in the flesh,
>> vindicated by the Spirit,
>>> seen by angels,
>> proclaimed among the nations,
>>> believed on in the world,
>>>> taken up in glory. (1 Tim. 3:16)

Our confession begins with the central fact of history: that God was manifested in the flesh! This confession was, and still is, a stumbling stone to many, but to Christians it is the foundation and joy of our confession:

> Who did leave his Father's throne
> To assume thy flesh and bone?
> Had He life or had He none?
>
> If He had not liv'd for thee,
> Thou hadst died most wretchedly
> And two deaths had been thy fee.
>
> —George Herbert[2]

This is what we confess. The alternative, to deny that God was manifested in the flesh in the person of Christ, will ultimately land people in a type of atheism, asking, Does God really care? The incarnation proves that God does care—enough for the Son to die for our sins.

Our confession is built on historical facts, not made-up fantasy. Jesus was manifested in a real town, of little significance, called Nazareth. This was a small town of farmers, which explains why so many of Jesus's sayings and parables reveal an intimate knowledge of his rural agricultural upbringing. Jesus himself, a "carpenter," probably worked with wood or stone, following the trade of his father, Joseph. But some scholars believe Jesus may also have worked on a family farm. He belonged to pious, God-fearing parents who worshiped in the synagogue and cultivated a piety that included daily prayers as well as Sabbath worship in the synagogue. And yet, we confess, the eternal Son of God was manifested in the flesh in these very ordinary circumstances.

A real human, needing the basic necessities of life, Jesus knew what it was to hunger and thirst, to rejoice and to weep, and to experience shame, suffering, and loneliness. His actions were often interpreted in the worst possible light, even though he healed people of diseases and delivered them from demons. He clearly enjoyed people, though many people did not enjoy him. But most of all, he lived as a man who truly honored and loved the God of Israel.

Incarnation

The Christian faith in its most basic form dies without the incarnation yet lives because the incarnate one dies. The idea of incarnation seems absurd to many, but in light of the Old Testament, it makes perfect sense. There are a number of ways the Son fulfills, in his enfleshment, the idea of God dwelling among his people from Old Testament patterns, images, and promises.

In Isaiah 55:10–11, God's word comes down from heaven, like the rain and the snow, to accomplish God's purposes. The Son of God, the Word in John 1, makes the same descent. The temple also was the place where God dwelled. Jesus's body is the new temple (John 2:19–21; Eph. 2:19–22) and the new tabernacle (John 1:14; Acts 15:16–17). He is the angel of the Lord, leading the people by the cloud of the Spirit (Rom. 8:14). He is the fulfillment of wisdom (1 Cor. 1:24), Torah (Rom. 10:4), and word (John 1:1–18). The Gospels are all about Jesus's reconstitution of Israel around himself. The ways and manner in which God dwelled among his people in the Old Testament are all fulfilled in the Son. All this is to say, the incarnation makes sense in light of God's manner of dealing with his people before the great event of the actual incarnation of the eternal Son. So much was pointing to God becoming flesh that only our sinful, darkened minds could miss it—and many in Christ's day did exactly that.

The major task concerning the person of Christ that we face as Christians seems to be identifying the manner in which we should understand his two natures in relation to him as one person. Jesus has a human nature and a divine nature, both of which, for our sake, are as important as the other. His divine nature is infinite, but his human nature is finite (i.e., limited)—and always will be. The human nature assumed by the eternal Son has an identity only at the moment of the incarnation; otherwise, there are two persons. As such, when referring to the person of Christ, we are speaking of the God-man, who possesses two natures: divine and human. But his divine nature is not his soul; rather, as a true human, he possesses both a body and a soul. The Westminster Shorter Catechism (q. 22) summarizes this well in stating that Christ "became man, by taking to himself a true body and a reasonable soul, being conceived by the power of the Holy Ghost in the womb of the virgin Mary, and born of her, yet without sin."

With this truth we can begin to understand some very important aspects of Christ's work on our behalf. The Westminster

Confession of Faith speaks of Christ's natures in relation to his work in the following way:

> Christ, in the work of mediation, acts according to both natures, by each nature doing that which is proper to itself; yet, by reason of the unity of the person, that which is proper to one nature is sometimes in Scripture attributed to the person denominated by the other nature. (8.7)

What Christians need to know, at the very least, is this: the God-man (singular person) acts according to both natures. Natures do not do anything on their own, as if we can say that the human nature died and the divine nature worked miracles. The work of Christ is the work of the God-man, not the work of natures in the abstract. This helps us understand a passage like Acts 20:28, "Pay careful attention to yourselves and to all the flock, in which the Holy Spirit has made you overseers, to care for the church of God, which he obtained with his own blood."

The blood of God purchased the church. Now since God is a spirit, we know that God does not have blood. But we also know that the eternal Son of God became flesh. Consequently, based on a doctrine called the *communication of properties*, we may affirm that God died because the work of Christ is attributed to the whole person, not to a specific nature. This communication does not mean that the human and divine natures are mixed but simply that what can be ascribed to either nature can be ascribed to the whole person. We can say that (the Son of) God died because we know that the God-man (a person) died, according to the human nature. The apostle Paul opens the book of Romans stating this truth, namely, that the (eternal) Son "was descended from David according to the flesh" (Rom. 1:3). He speaks of a singular person but highlights a specific nature.

The God-man is indeed the mystery that we love to confess. We are talking about a person who can have an infinite glory and a finite grief, one who has eternally unchangeable happiness and blessedness but overwhelming sorrow that led to weeping, one who upholds the world by his power but was upheld in his mother's arms, one who created all the world's waters but said, "I thirst." More poetically, Augustine's words express the wonder of the God-man:

> Man's maker was made man,
> that He, Ruler of the stars, might nurse at His mother's
> breast;
> that the Bread might hunger,
> the Fountain thirst,
> the Light sleep,
> the Way be tired on its journey;
> that the Truth might be accused of false witness,
> the Teacher be beaten with whips,
> the Foundation be suspended on wood;
> that Strength might grow weak;
> that the Healer might be wounded;
> that Life might die.[3]

One cannot make sense of Augustine's theological poetry apart from the person of Christ. With knowledge of the God-man, however, everything he writes about our Lord is truth upon truth.

The Anointed One

That Yahweh became flesh would be blasphemous, if it were false. On the contrary, it truly occurred and so is glorious. Yet he was not a human without a historical context. His name is Jesus

(Gk. for Joshua, meaning "Savior"). He was a historical person, born of the Virgin Mary, who for most of his life studied and labored but for roughly three years exercised an itinerant ministry that shook the world around him and subsequently changed the course of world history. This is precisely what the promised Messiah was supposed to do (Ps. 110:1; Isa. 53:10–12).

His full name is not Jesus Christ, unless you understand Christ as a reference to his "trade." When understood this way, Jesus is the Christ, the anointed one, the Jewish Messiah. Speaking to the Gentiles, Peter gives a crystallized understanding of the person who has brought good news to the world:

> As for the word that he sent to Israel, preaching good news of peace through Jesus Christ (he is Lord of all), you yourselves know what happened throughout all Judea, beginning from Galilee after the baptism that John proclaimed: how God anointed Jesus of Nazareth with the Holy Spirit and with power. He went about doing good and healing all who were oppressed by the devil, for God was with him. (Acts 10:36–38)

Jesus is the Lord of all, not just of Israel. We know this for one simple reason: God was with him; the Father anointed his Son with the Holy Spirit. As such, the Son was able to defeat the powers of darkness, including the devil (Heb. 2:14). Importantly, the coming of Jesus was also the coming of the Spirit in a unique manner. This connection requires explanation, for the heart of our salvation is intimately tied to the relationship between Jesus and the Spirit.

In the Old Testament prophecies about God's relationship to his servant, the Messiah, we are told explicitly that God will uphold him by putting his Spirit on him:

> Behold my servant, whom I uphold,
>> my chosen, in whom my soul delights;
> I have put my Spirit upon him;
>> he will bring forth justice to the nations. (Isa. 42:1)

Not surprisingly, then, the Gospel accounts of Jesus's life have a strong focus on the manner in which Yahweh was with Jesus, namely, by the powerful indwelling of the Holy Spirit. This work begins at the incarnation, whereby the Spirit is the divine efficient cause of the formation of the Son's human nature in the womb (Matt. 1:18, 20; Luke 1:35). As the prophecies about God's servant from Isaiah (Isa. 42:1; 61:1) unfold in the life of Jesus, we note that our Lord received the Spirit without measure (John 3:34), and at his baptism the Spirit descended (publicly) on him and into him (see Mark 1:10, where the Greek literally means "the Spirit was descending into him").

The whole of Christ's ministry can be summed up in seven simple words: *he did the will of the Father*. The Father, who pours out the Spirit on his Son, uses the Spirit to guide Jesus in a most forceful way at times. Consider the language of Mark 1:12: "The Spirit immediately *drove* him out into the wilderness." After Christ's temptation in the wilderness and his successful binding of Satan, he returns to his public ministry in power (Luke 4:14–15). Sadly, in Nazareth, his sermon is rejected—a sermon from Isaiah 61:1–2 ("the Spirit of the Lord GOD is upon me"), in which Christ spoke of God's grace not only to Jews but also to Gentiles (Luke 4:16–27). Not only that, but the miracles that Christ performs are done in the power of the Spirit (Matt. 12:18; Acts 10:38). Even his offering up of himself on the cross is done in the power of the Spirit (Heb. 9:14). Just as he is able to lay down his life by the Spirit, so the resurrection is attributed to the Holy Spirit (Rom. 8:11), and it is in his resurrection that Jesus is declared "to be the Son of God . . . according to the Spirit of holiness" (Rom. 1:4; see also 1 Tim. 3:16; 1 Pet. 3:18).

Why is this important? In short, we are talking about a person who, though fully divine, did not consider equality with God something to be exploited. Rather, the Son's coming into this world and assuming to himself a true human nature was an entrance that would mean that the eternal Son would also be the dependent Son in every way.

The work of the Spirit on Jesus, especially concerning the perfecting in him of faith, hope, and love, became the pattern by which the same Spirit does his work on those united to Christ. Without the Spirit's work on and in Christ, the foundation for the Spirit's work on and in us disintegrates.

In terms of the Spirit's work in us, his goal is to stamp the moral character of Jesus on our renewed human nature. After all, this is what Paul says is the purpose of our predestination: "For those whom [God the Father] foreknew he also predestined to be conformed to the image of his Son" (Rom. 8:29). This is, of course, a corporate goal of God's, which he accomplishes through the two greatest gifts he can give to us: his Son and the Spirit.

In other words, Christianity needs to be focused not simply on Christ but more precisely on the Spirit of Christ (Rom. 8:9; 1 Pet. 1:11). Who is Jesus? Jesus is the man of the Spirit *par excellence*. And his possession of the Spirit (2 Cor. 3:17) is the reason his people experience the same. Let us not miss this amazing fact: the very Spirit who dwelled on and in Christ is the same who dwells on and in us.

With Authority

As the one who is fully God and fully man, empowered by the Spirit, the Father's representative prophet, priest, and king, Jesus has an authority that gives significance to his saving work. When he preached, John records, Jesus preached with authority, causing those who listened to him to say, "No one ever spoke like this man!" (John 7:46). Matthew likewise writes, "And when Jesus finished these sayings, the crowds were astonished at his teaching, for he was teaching them as one who had authority, and not as their scribes" (Matt. 7:28–29).

His healing ministry was another sign of his authority. When Jesus forgave the sins of a paralytic (Matt. 9:1–8), the people, of course, responded by accusing him of blasphemy. But knowing their thoughts, probably through a revelation given by the Spirit, Jesus performed a miracle in plain view so that they might know that he had authority to forgive sins. After the healing, the crowds glorified God for giving authority to this man.

To be the mouthpiece of God on earth, Jesus had to have received full authority from God. Jesus was not shy about his authority, saying in one place, "All things have been handed over to me by my Father, and no one knows the Son except the Father, and no one knows the Father except the Son" (Matt. 11:27). This theme runs right through Matthew's Gospel, culminating in the Great Commission, when Jesus publicly told his apostles, "All authority in heaven and on earth has been given to me" (Matt. 28:18). As the second Adam, who succeeded where the first Adam miserably failed, Jesus was tasked with "being fruitful and multiplying" (cf. Gen. 1:28). His apostles were tasked with going and making God-fearing disciples throughout the world who would receive power from Christ himself to accomplish the goal of populating the earth with children of God.

Now this emphasis on authority is not without reason. Who ultimately has authority on earth right now? The answer: Jesus of Nazareth, who has been raised from the dead and now sits at the right hand of God in power and authority. Jesus runs the church, saves sinners, and rules with absolute authority as king. Modern "Christian" liberalism cannot and does not give to Christ what is rightfully his: supreme authority in heaven and on earth. For the liberal, Jesus is merely a spectacle of the ideal human being who loved others. In truth, he is far more than that. He is the one who loved so much that he laid down his life for sinners (being "crucified in weakness," 2 Cor. 13:4), but he is also the one who freely gave up his life as an authoritative king and then was resurrected to a life of power and glory.

5

Prophet, Priest, and King

Why do we bother ourselves with learning about Christ's person and work? As Christians, we have come to believe that he is worth studying and knowing (John 17:3). In his justly famous *Institutes of the Christian Religion*, John Calvin writes,

> The name of Jesus is not only light but also food; it is also oil, without which all food of the soul is dry; it is salt, without whose seasoning whatever is set before us is insipid; finally, it is honey in the mouth, melody in the ear, rejoicing in the heart, and at the same time medicine. Every discourse in which his name is not spoken is without savor.[1]

Christians are deficient in understanding Christ's person if they fail to grasp his threefold office as prophet, priest, and king. Everything we need to know about Christ's work on behalf of sinners as the mediator between God and man can be subsumed under his threefold office. These are offices bestowed on him from above: God the Father called him, and his calling is wondrously fulfilled, which means Jesus is still now our prophet, priest, and king.

71

Prophet

God speaks to us. Deism miserably fails exactly on this point, since the deity merely "moved" (created) but does not continue to speak. On the contrary, Christianity depends on God speaking to us. God could have justly given the world he created the "silent treatment" after Adam and Eve sinned, but he continued to speak to those whom he loves with truths far too grand for us to understand naturally.

God speaks the world into existence, but he does not stop there. He is a communicative God, so that all true theology is ultimately relational theology. This explains why so many theologians have focused on the covenant concept—so obviously important in the Scriptures—because in God's speech to his people there are certain promises and rewards, as well as conditions and threats. These are the basic components of a covenantal relationship.

The pinnacle of God's speaking is the actual calling of his Son to the office of prophet in the context of a covenant between the two:

> You have said, "I have made a covenant with my
>   chosen one;
>   I have sworn to David my servant:
> 'I will establish your offspring forever,
>   and build your throne for all generations.'" *Selah*
>   (Ps. 89:3–4)

God establishes his Son's throne in various ways, especially by making him his mouthpiece on earth. Jesus is the prince of the prophets (Deut. 18:18), the chief shepherd of the church. As the writer of Hebrews notes, formerly "God spoke to our fathers by the prophets, but in these last days he has spoken

to us by his Son, whom he appointed the heir of all things"
(Heb. 1:1–2). The Father speaks through his Son. The servant
in Isaiah 49:1–2 calls for worldwide attention, noting that the
Lord called him from the womb and made his mouth "like a
sharp sword." Christ himself claims that "all things" have been
handed over to him by his Father, which is a result of his knowing the Father (Matt. 11:27). If he did not know the Father, he
would be utterly unable to declare perfectly and infallibly the
will of the Father. But because he knows the Father, in a way
that no other human ever has or ever will, Jesus can say, "I
have not spoken on my own authority, but the Father who sent
me has himself given me a commandment—what to say and
what to speak. . . . What I say, therefore, I say as the Father has
told me" (John 12:49–50).

With this peculiar privilege, Jesus gives light to the world
(John 1:9). He foretells and forthtells the words of God. No
man ever spoke like Jesus (John 7:46); no one has spoken with
such authority (Luke 4:32). As the preeminent prophet of the
church, Christ reveals the glories of salvation. As glorious as
Isaiah's words about Christ are—which, incidentally, still came
from Christ himself—there is no doubt that the Upper Room
Discourse (John 14–16) and Christ's so-called high priestly
prayer (John 17) are unparalleled disclosures of God's purposes
in salvation up to that point in redemptive history. The treasures
of wisdom and knowledge are in Christ (Col. 2:3), not to be hid-
den but to be revealed to those whom the Father has given to
his Son. One of his great privileges as the God-man is to declare
perfectly the revelation of the Father to us in a manner fitting to
our finite condition (Matt. 13:1–52; John 1:18).

The Father not only called Christ to his prophetic office
but also equipped him for it. His natural giftings and graces,

including a sinless nature, coupled with the fullness of the Spirit poured out on him, placed him in a unique position not only to learn from God but also to declare the purposes of God unlike any prophet before or after him could. The revelation of God's purposes by the God-man is the result of his truly human faculties apprehending the truth and delivering that same truth in a manner suitable to our condition.

What Christ knew and declared was derivative knowledge handed to him, according to his human nature, from above. He spoke no more than he was granted to know: "But concerning that day and hour no one knows, not even the angels of heaven, nor the Son, but the Father only" (Matt. 24:36). Christ, now exalted in the heavenly places, is no longer ignorant of his return. But he was, at one point, unaware of the day and hour of the second coming, because such prophetic knowledge had not been revealed to him in his state of humiliation. How humbling for the omniscient one not to "cheat" and depend on his own divine prerogatives but to humble himself to the point of being dependent on the Father for his knowledge.

There is a sense in which Christ's office as mediator will end with the consummation of all things (1 Cor. 15:24). Yet the "handing over" of the kingdom to the Father does not mean that Christ will not forever continue to be the mouthpiece of God. His glory as the God-man means he will ever remain the mediator of communications from God to the redeemed church, since there will always be a vast difference between us finite human beings (even in glory) and the infinite God. The truth about God that is suitable to our glorified humanity will be found in and proceed from the person of Christ. The man Christ Jesus will continually reveal God's glory and ongoing will for our lives in the new heavens and new earth (Rev. 22:1–4).[2]

This point, I think, is hugely significant for us as we consider whether God has more revelation for us as his people, even with the closing of the canon (i.e., the sixty-six books of the Bible). If God is going to speak to us, it will come from the lips of Christ himself. "Does God still speak to us today?" is a question some ask. But few care to ask, "Does God still speak to us today about his Son so that what we receive leads to his glory and a greater knowledge of the Savior?" This, it seems to me, is a more significant question than debating whether God has told a young man, somehow, to marry a good-looking, godly young lady who doesn't yet know his last name.

We can say, on the one hand, that God has spoken to us in his word through Christ and that the words of eternal life are sealed on our hearts through the Spirit. But we can also say, on the other hand, that God has more to say to us about himself through Christ. I tend to think, however, that, ordinarily speaking, this new knowledge and revelation is something we wait for in the age when we no longer walk by faith but instead live by sight. Only then can we be certain that Christ is speaking to us.

Priest

If we have any confidence before God, it is a direct result of Christ's priesthood. The chief purpose of his priesthood was not simply to offer himself but to bring us to God. One needs to keep in mind that if Christ's prophetic office highlights God's words to us, his priestly office highlights Christ's words to God on our behalf. If you could ask God one thing for yourself, what would you ask? The truth is, Christ speaks the very best words to the Father on your behalf because he is a faithful high priest.

Christ was called to the priesthood by God (Heb. 5:5). However, he was not an Aaronic priest. Rather, he belonged to the order of Melchizedek (Heb. 5:6, 10), the mysterious priest-king spoken of in Genesis 14:18–20 and Psalm 110:4. God called him to a life of suffering, which culminated in Christ offering himself as a lamb without blemish for the sins of his people. The fruits of his death for the sake of his people are applied to us only because Christ himself intercedes as the risen Savior in the heavenly places. As for foundational Christianity, no one disputes the central place Christ's death has in God's purposes to save sinners, but many neglect to realize that Christ's intercession is as important as his oblation (i.e., his offering himself unto death).

The death of Christ and his resulting intercession are really two sides of the same coin. Neither has any significance for us apart from the other. If Christ does not intercede for us, we are without hope and without God for us. But if he utters our name, even once, we are as good as glorified. Jesus has received all authority in heaven and on earth and intercedes as a faithful Son in the presence of his Father (Heb. 7:25). Just as the Son delights to bring our names to the Father, so the Father delights to hear our names and answer Christ's requests.

Moreover, Christ's intercession is so closely tied to his death that in his presence before the Father, Jesus continually presents the efficacy or completeness of his death in our defense. There is no sense at all in which the Son must "twist the arm" of the Father. Rather, according to the justice, goodness, faithfulness, and promise of God, the Son's intercession is part of the triune God's resolve to save sinners in a manner consistent with his nature and for the promotion of his glory.

Integral to our understanding of Christ's priestly work is our affirmation of his two natures. To be a priest, the Messiah must be a man. If he is not a true human being, with a body and soul, he cannot possibly offer himself up on the cross in a meaningful way as our representative. In fact, to be a merciful high priest, he must be able to sympathize with people in their weaknesses (Heb. 4:15). While Christ's ministry was concentrated to a few years in his thirties after he was baptized and publicly ordained, there is a profound sense in which his whole life was a sort of oblation (i.e., an offering of himself). He was tried and tested his whole life to be able to minister to those who would be tried and tested during their lives.

Our Lord is not, however, simply a man, though he is a man. He is also fully divine, and so the identity of his person is that of God-man. As such, his person has infinite worth. Humans cannot merit anything before God, but the God-man, according to the promises made by the Father, can perform a work that God rewards. If Jesus were simply a man, his death could save only one sinner, but because he is the God-man, his death is able to save a multitude of sinners. The worth of his person gives worth to his actions. Accordingly, in Acts 20:28, we are told that the church is purchased by the blood of God. The God-man, not a nature, died.

Our great high priest shared in flesh and blood (Heb. 2:17–18). He offered prayers for himself and for our sake "with loud cries and tears" (Heb. 5:7). His prayers were a testimony not only to his ongoing priestly work but also to the willing but difficult obedience he offered up to the Father in our place. Jesus willingly subjected himself to the curse of the law and so had to die a cursed death (Gal. 3:13). During his life of humiliation on earth, he experienced constant suffering to learn obedience (Heb. 5:8). He died in a manner that was not altogether inconsistent with how he lived: in shame. But regardless of how the

Jewish religious intelligentsia viewed him, in the eyes of the Father, the one who ultimately matters, the death of Christ was a fragrant offering and sacrifice to God (Eph. 5:2).

As a priest, Jesus lived and died and rose again as a "common person." Jesus is described as "holy, innocent, unstained, separated from sinners, and exalted above the heavens" (Heb. 7:26). So he could not have laid down his life purely for himself; he had to be mediating on our behalf. And not only in the book of Hebrews but also in the book of Romans (esp. chaps. 3–5), there is a strong substitutionary element to the work of Christ as the propitiation for our sins. The Father gives to Christ a people (John 6:39), and Christ lives, dies, and rises for their sake as well as his own (John 15:10). But when he intercedes in heaven, he is interceding on our behalf.

As the Old Testament plainly teaches, the high priest entered the Most Holy Place not for himself but for the people. Thus, he was commanded to have the names of the twelve tribes on his shoulders (Ex. 28:21). Christ died with the "twelve tribes" on his shoulders: his elect people. But for all this talk of suffering and death, we must not miss something crucial: it was a victorious death. He defeated the serpent, the devil, who had the power of death, and so Jesus is the true Joshua who delivers his people (Heb. 2:14–15).

King

The Jewish people desired a messiah to take center stage in their liberation from Rome, a messiah who, from the line of David, would give Israel a military victory. At times during Jesus's ministry, the Jewish people wanted to make him their king (John 6:15). The Roman authorities even killed Jesus for being the "King of the Jews" (e.g., Matt. 27:37).

Now Jesus was descended from David, and he does take center stage and does provide liberation for Israel—but on God's terms. As the king of the world, he subdues his people to himself, rules them by his law, and defends them. The New Testament authors were not shy about driving home to their readers the importance of showing that Jesus of Nazareth is the Son of God who fulfills the Old Testament prophecies of a promised king who would rule the world. In fact, the most quoted Old Testament verse that is applied to Jesus, if we consider both explicit and implicit references, comes from Psalm 110:1. At the right hand of the Father is Jesus, who subdues his enemies:

> The LORD says to my Lord:
> "Sit at my right hand,
> until I make your enemies your footstool."

Christ as king is not a reference to his divine nature alone. Rather, as the king of Israel who will rule the world, he must be a human king. Consider the way Paul opens his letter to the Romans,

> Paul, a servant of Christ Jesus, called to be an apostle, set apart for the gospel of God, which he promised beforehand through his prophets in the holy Scriptures, concerning his Son, who was descended from David according to the flesh and was declared to be the Son of God in power according to the Spirit of holiness by his resurrection from the dead, Jesus Christ our Lord. (Rom. 1:1–4)

This is actually kingly language used by Paul to describe Jesus. Jesus fulfills the Old Testament prophecies that a descendant of David would rule the world, and by the resurrection of the dead, we know Jesus is the Son of God and Lord of the world (2 Sam. 7:12–16; Ps. 89; Ezek. 34:23–24). As the mediator, Christ is king. He is king in his state of humiliation (i.e., cradle to the grave) and in his state of exaltation (i.e., resurrection onward).

In fact, two psalms (Pss. 2; 110) highlight the two states of Christ in relation to his kingship. Both psalms speak of the nations being subdued (Pss. 2:1–3; 110:1–2), the destruction of Israel's enemies (Pss. 2:9; 110:5–6), and God's wrath against the enemies of the Son (Pss. 2:5; 110:5–6). The Son of God, a kingly title (see Matt. 16:16), is Jesus of Nazareth. In Psalm 110 there are subtle shifts from the emphases in Psalm 2. In Psalm 110, Christ is seated at the right hand of the Father (Ps. 110:1, 5; cf. Col. 3:1; Heb. 1:3). He is enthroned and has all power and authority (Ps. 110:1–2, 5–6; cf. Matt. 28:18); he has all honor and favor that can be given to a man. The differences in the two psalms become apparent when considering Christ's transition from "weakness" to "power": in Psalm 2:2 the "rulers take counsel together, against the LORD and against his Anointed," but in Psalm 110:2 Christ rules in the midst of his enemies. In addition, in Psalm 2:8 the Son asks for the nations as his inheritance, but in Psalm 110 God uses Christ's rule to fight for his Son. The rulers and nations were summoned to submit to God's Son in Psalm 2:10–12, but because they did not submit, the wrathful outcome is highlighted in Psalm 110:5–6.

In the New Testament, Christ himself uses Psalm 110:1 to speak of his transcendence and lordship over David (Mark 12:36–37), even though he is fully aware that he descended from David. Peter also references Psalm 110:1 when speaking of Christ's vindication after the resurrection (Acts 2:32–36). Besides Jesus and Peter, Paul also alludes to Psalm 110 in Romans 8:34 as he connects Christ's kingship with his (priestly) intercession: "Who is to condemn? Christ Jesus is the one who died—more than that, who was raised—who is at the right hand of God, who indeed is interceding for us." All this is to say, there is no doubt that Jesus, the Lord of glory, is the one who has lordship over all creatures.

Summing Up

Jesus is the second Adam, who subdues the world to himself (see Ps. 8; Heb. 2:5–9). For those of us who are united to Jesus, we will share in this cosmic victory; we will judge the angels (1 Cor. 6:3); we will inherit the earth, the new Eden; we will inherit what Christ inherits because we are his bride and bear his name (Rev. 3:12). The oil of anointing on his head (Ps. 45:7) is the oil we receive: the promised Holy Spirit. We also share in the access Christ has to the Father's presence. As our priest-king, Christ brings us into the Most Holy Place, where he will continue, as our prophet, to speak good things to us for all eternity and where, as our king, he will defend and protect us.

In his penetrating work *Christ's Exaltation Purchased by Humiliation*, the Puritan Richard Sibbes offers us a rather appropriate way to meditate on our mediator now that he is in glory:

> Oh it is a sweet meditation, beloved, to think that our flesh is now in heaven, at the right hand of God; and that flesh that was born of the virgin, that was laid in the manger, that went up and down doing good, that was made a curse for us and humbled to death, and lay under the bondage of death three days; that this flesh is now glorious in heaven, that this person is Lord over the living and the dead. It is an excellent book to study this. Beloved, study Christ in the state of humiliation and exaltation.[3]

All our confidence and assurance before God is dependent on the realities that Christ, for our sake, became a prophet, priest, and king and remains such now in glory. Christianity, if it is to be pure and consistent with the pattern of the Scriptures, must be a Christianity that focuses on the person of Christ before his work. Who is the Christ, the Son of God?

> Who is this King of glory?
>   The LORD of hosts,
>   he is the King of glory! *Selah* (Ps. 24:10)

The Son of God who passed through the heavens as the victorious prophet, priest, and king—he is the "King of glory"; he is the "LORD of hosts."

6

Life and Death

The Christian faith sounds rather absurd when one thinks about the claims it makes. Over two thousand years ago, a Jewish man, declaring himself to be Israel's Messiah, who also happens to be the second person of the Trinity, died at the hands of the Roman civic authorities, with no little help from his own Jewish people, who by and large condemned him, and this death on a cross was ultimately the means God used to defeat the devil and deal with the sins of the world. More than that, this Jewish man, named Jesus (of Nazareth), was raised from the dead and currently rules the world from his position as the enthroned King of kings and Lord of lords. More poetically, when Jesus knew that it was not God's will for the cup to pass from him, he held on to it out of love to his Father, but he also drank the full measure of it out of love to us. And his drinking that cup is what satisfies our thirst. "Outlandish!" cry many.

But on closer reflection, the story is rather beautiful. God does not sit in the heavenly places and utter pious platitudes to us that, despite our misery, all will work out in the end and we just need to have some faith. Rather, the triune God determined that the divine Son would be "born of a woman, born under law, to redeem those who were under the law" (Gal. 4:4–5). And in his coming to earth, the Son entered into the sin and misery of this world by living a life filled with grief and suffering; he was humiliated in every way so that he might be a Savior who can appreciate and sympathize with us who experience various degrees of sufferings and miseries in this world. God has provided people with the one thing they need: a Savior who brings forgiveness and reconciliation. It is a universal message because it has a universal application to every human being who has sinned and fallen short of God's glory.

A "Common Person"

Jesus lived on earth as a "common person"—a term that older Reformed theologians used to indicate his role as our representative. As mediator and surety, he took on the role of a "common person" because of the relationship he has with the Father. The Father gave a people to Jesus (John 17:6), who are Christ's sheep (John 10:15–16). Thus, we are those who are chosen in Christ in eternity (Eph. 1:4), which is another manner of highlighting that Jesus was and is a "common person," acting on our behalf as our representative. Since this is true, the eternal Son did not owe his life and suffering to God—how could that be so?—but rather, as mediator on behalf of the elect, he voluntarily undertook human flesh and suffering based on the (eternal) plan of salvation decreed by the Godhead (John 17; Phil. 2:6–11).

The Son, coming into the world, undertook for our sakes not only to obey but also to suffer what was required of us and then to intercede on behalf of us. As a "common person," one who identified fully with us, Jesus, being raised from the dead, was in a position (raised "in power," Rom. 1:4) to bestow on his bride all the fruits of his death. We are thus reconciled with God through Jesus (Rom. 5:8–11), after having been separated from fellowship with God through the sin of Adam, who himself was a "common person," or representative (Rom. 5; see also 2 Cor. 5:21; Gal. 3:13; 1 Pet. 2:21, 24).

The language of "common person" reflects the popular concept that Christ is our substitute. While some have questioned the idea that Jesus acted as the substitute of his people, it is fairly hard to read the book of Romans without getting the impression that Christ's death for our sakes was substitutionary. He went to the cross, willingly, so that we might have a crown. He shrieked with cries of abandonment so that we might sing with cries of joy. This makes sense, of course, only if he is our substitute. As Stephen Charnock eloquently testified hundreds of years ago,

> He received our evils to bestow his good, and submitted to our curse to impart to us his blessings; sustained the extremity of that wrath we had deserved, to confer upon us the grace he had purchased. The sin in us, which he was free from, was by divine estimation transferred upon him, as if he were guilty, that the righteousness he has, which we were destitute of, might be transferred upon us, as if we were innocent. He was made sin, as if he had sinned all the sins of men, and we are made righteousness, as if we had not sinned at all.[1]

Substitution denotes a context in which one takes the place of another. But we have, in Christ, the substitute who not only took our place and thus received what we deserved but also gave us what he alone deserves. Essential Christianity is substitutionary Christianity: the one in the place of others for their good. One, who being very nature God, did not consider equality with

God something to be exploited or taken advantage of but freely made himself nothing for our sakes (Phil. 2:6–7).

Hence, we who died with Christ will live and reign with him (2 Tim. 2:11–12); we have been crucified with Christ (Gal. 2:20) and buried with him in baptism (Rom. 6:4). Based on our union with him, if we were buried with him, we will also be raised with him (Col. 2:12–13; 3:1). In fact, God has made us alive with him and "raised us up with him and seated us with him in the heavenly places" (Eph. 2:6). In other words, because he is a "common person," acting as our substitute, whatever is true of him becomes, in a manner of speaking, true of us. Where he goes, we go!

Active and Passive Obedience

Christ's obedience for our sakes has reference to three major "parts" of his mediatorial office: his lifelong obedience, the suffering of the cross, and his heavenly intercession.[2] All three are necessary aspects of his duty toward God the Father. And all three form the basis for the blessings we receive from his hand.

In the obedience of his life, Jesus willingly, perpetually, and perfectly conformed his heart, soul, mind, and strength (i.e., his will) to the will of God. The Scriptures frequently and clearly testify to the obedient servant, who is the fulfillment of the Old Testament prophecies that God's Messiah ("servant," Isa. 42:1) would be the fully obedient one:

> The Lord GOD has given me
>   the tongue of those who are taught,
> that I may know how to sustain with a word
>   him who is weary.
> Morning by morning he awakens;
>   he awakens my ear
>   to hear as those who are taught.

The Lord GOD has opened my ear,
and I was not rebellious;
I turned not backward.
I gave my back to those who strike,
and my cheeks to those who pull out the beard;
I hid not my face
from disgrace and spitting. (Isa. 50:4–6)

As God's faithful Son (Ps. 2), he learned obedience through his sufferings (Heb. 5:8). In the great "hymn" in Philippians 2, Paul writes, "And being found in human form, he humbled himself by becoming obedient to the point of death, even death on a cross" (Phil. 2:8). The great motivation for Christ to remain obedient was not only to save his people (Isa. 53) but also to remain in the Father's love (John 15:10). Could there be any greater motive for obedience than to remain in the Father's love?

What precisely was the nature of Christ's obedience in his human nature? John Owen refers to it as "the absolute, complete, exact conformity of the soul of Christ to the will, mind, or law of God."[3] He adds, "The *actual* obedience of Christ . . . was his willing, cheerful, obedient performance of every thing, duty, or command, that God, by virtue of any law whereto we were subject and obnoxious, did require."[4] As such, God sent his Son, "born of woman, born under the law, to redeem those who were under the law, so that we might receive adoption as sons" (Gal. 4:4–5).

In terms of Christ's obedience, theologians have often spoken of the twofold relationship Jesus had to the commands or will of God: (1) his duty, as an Israelite, born under the law, to fulfill not only the moral law but also the ceremonial laws and the civil laws of the land, so long as the latter did not require him to break God's law (which always takes precedence);

and (2) the law placed on him as mediator, which was for him alone, such as God requiring Jesus to lay down his life, as seen in John 10:18: "No one takes [my life] from me, but I lay it down of my own accord. I have authority to lay it down, and I have authority to take it up again. This charge I have received from my Father."

The quality of Christ's obedience to the Father was extensively and intensively perfect. He not only obeyed the entire law of God, but he did so in a manner impossible for any other creature. Indeed, we might argue that Jesus could have died as a sacrifice shortly after the incarnation and that that would be sufficient for the removal of our sins. But there is a reason he lived as long as he did in the circumstances placed on him by the Father, namely, that his "active" obedience was not only for his sake (i.e., that he may glorify himself and his Father) but also for our sake (i.e., that we may receive his righteousness). After all, Jesus obeyed not merely the law of nature, as Adam was bound to, but also the various laws associated with the ceremonies of Israel that typified holiness and the removal of sins.

His so-called "passive obedience" should also be clearly understood. John Murray, in his excellent work *Redemption Accomplished and Applied*, argues that we cannot assign certain acts of Jesus to the category of "active obedience" and other acts to the category of "passive obedience." The distinction is not really about periods in our Lord's life (i.e., from the womb to the garden; from the garden to the tomb). Rather, as Murray says, "The real use and purpose of the formula is to emphasize the two distinct aspects of our Lord's vicarious obedience."[5] He adds,

> The truth expressed rests upon the recognition that the law of God has both penal sanctions and positive demands. It

demands not only the full discharge of its precepts but also the infliction of penalty for all infractions and shortcomings. It is this twofold demand of the law of God which is taken into account when we speak of the active and passive obedience of Christ.[6]

Who can really deny that Jesus was very much "active" in his offering up himself on the cross, which he did willingly in obedience to the Father? His whole life was a life of suffering ("passive obedience"), but his whole life was also a life of serving the Father to the point of death ("active obedience"). When understood this way, the distinction between his "active" and "passive" obedience seems less artificial and more in keeping with the various aspects of what it meant to be God's suffering servant. Thus, his righteousness that is credited (imputed) to us is his whole obedience, which includes his suffering obedience, since you cannot really divorce the parts of Christ's life from each other. In connection with this, as John Calvin notes, "For this reason the so-called 'Apostles' Creed' passes at once in the best order from the birth of Christ to his death and resurrection, wherein the whole of perfect salvation consists. Yet the remainder of the obedience that he manifested in his life is not excluded."[7]

The Sacrificial Lamb

What is the biblical understanding of a sacrifice offered to God? The well-regarded Reformed theologian Johannes Cloppenburg (1592–1652) calls a sacrifice a "religious oblation [i.e., offering] of something consecrated and dedicated to God, by the ministry of a priest, according to God's institution, to be destroyed, for a testimony of the worship of God and an external symbol."[8] This is about the best summary I have come across regarding the nature of a true sacrifice and, in particular, what it means for our Lord to be considered a sacrifice.[9]

But was Christ "destroyed"? In one sense, yes. But in another sense, no, he was not. The person of Christ was not destroyed, nor could he be. The union of his two natures remains even after death. True, Christ's body-soul was sacrificed on the cross, but it was his body that was killed—and then his soul departed. So by "destroyed" we mean that his body lost life and his soul departed.[10] But while Christ died on the cross according to his human nature, his death was still of infinite value to satisfy God's justice and thus secure the forgiveness of his people because the (singular) person sacrificing is infinite (Heb. 1:1–3; 2:17–18; 9:9–14, 22–28). He is the God-man (*theánthrōpos*), the sacrificial Lamb.

Whatever John the Baptist may have meant in John 1:29 ("Behold, the Lamb of God, who takes away the sin of the world"), he likely understood, to some degree, that Jesus would be an atoning sacrifice. Perhaps John even had in mind the lamb of Isaiah 53:7, since John was clearly familiar with the book of Isaiah:

> He was oppressed, and he was afflicted,
>> yet he opened not his mouth;
> like a lamb that is led to the slaughter,
>> and like a sheep that before its shearers is silent,
>> so he opened not his mouth.

The Greek translation of the Old Testament (i.e., the Septuagint) uses the word *amnos* ("lamb"), which is also used in John 1:29. God provides a Lamb, and it is Jesus.

The Levitical sacrifices, in fact, were patterned on a heavenly exemplar (Heb. 9:23–28). The sacrificial blood offerings of Leviticus foreshadowed the sacrificial blood offering of Christ, since animal offerings could never satisfy the severity of God's justice or the purity of his infinite holiness. Yet the "blood" aspect foreshadowed in the Old Testament reveals something of the nature of Christ's sacrifice in terms of what it means not only for us but for God.

Propitiation

All forgiveness is based on propitiation. We have committed crimes against God. As Isaiah says of us and of the solution to our problem,

> All we like sheep have gone astray;
>> we have turned—every one—to his own way;
> and the LORD has laid on him
>> the iniquity of us all. (Isa. 53:6)

The Lord God laid on Christ our iniquity, thus reconciling us to himself (Rom. 5:10; Eph. 2:13; Col. 1:20–23). Christ's death has a certain forensic meaning: God reveals his vindicatory righteousness and thus justifies those who have faith in his Son (Rom. 3:25–26).

In Romans 3:25 Paul speaks of God putting forward his Son as a propitiation by his blood. Christ's sacrifice is propitiatory (see also Rom. 5:9; 1 Cor. 11:25; Eph. 5:2). This is a hard concept for many today. If we grant that Christ's death served as a propitiation, then we are affirming that his sacrifice satisfied God's wrath, which means God possesses a righteous wrath against mankind that only Christ's death can appease. Propitiation is not simply expiation (wiping away sin) but the appeasing of God's righteous wrath so that, through Christ, we might receive God's favor.

For those wishing to dispense with the idea of a wrathful God, Romans 3:25 is not a place of refuge. In Paul's letter to the

Romans, he has already spoken of the wrath of God against ungodliness (Rom. 1:18) and also of wrath on those who judge others but do the very same things, thus storing up for themselves wrath on the day of God's wrath (2:3, 5). So when we speak of propitiation, we are doing justice to the overall theme of Paul's theology in Romans. Let it be said, however, that the giving of Christ is evidence that God gave in love, so we are talking about a just God who gives Christ in love so that he does not have to be wrathful toward his people (Eph. 2:3–4). Thus the "cup" Christ asks to be removed from him in the garden of Gethsemane, though one that he submits to drinking, is the cup of God's wrath (Ps. 75:8; Isa. 51:17, 22; Jer. 25:15–17, 28–29; 49:12; Rev. 14:10; 16:19).

Many great people have been exalted because of their lives, but Jesus is valued, above all, for his death. Mercy and righteousness, wrath and grace, punishment and forgiveness, God and man find reconciliation in the one who, for our sakes, cried out so that we might never have to utter his cry of loneliness.

Conclusion

H. Richard Niebuhr memorably described the liberal Christianity of the mid-twentieth century as follows: "A God without wrath brought men without sin into a kingdom without judgment through the ministrations of a Christ without a cross."[11] Conversely, Christianity asserts that a God, who could justly execute wrath on humanity, sent his Son into the world to obey and suffer as a propitiatory sacrifice on behalf of those who deserved wrath but, through faith, receive the opposite. But the story of the God-man, *theánthrōpos*, does not end at the cross. For if it did, you have already read too far in this book, and all I can suggest is Paul's advice that if Christ and the dead are not raised, "Let us eat and drink, for tomorrow we die" (1 Cor. 15:32).

7

Exaltation

Jesus desires for us what he desired for himself: exaltation. He would not be a good groom to his bride if that were not the case. But he knew, better than we can possibly know, that true exaltation comes through humility (Matt. 23:12). We can accept this principle as true, but practicing it is an altogether different story.

Gregory of Nazianzus once remarked of Jesus, "He assumes the poverty of my flesh that I might inherit the riches of His Godhead."[1] No one has sunk so low from such a lofty place as Jesus. His sinking was, in part, why so many did not and could not recognize him for who he is. He sank, lower and lower, humiliated in every way, to the point of death, even death on a cross (Phil. 2:7–8). Yet no one has been raised so high from such a low place as the Lord of glory (Phil. 2:9–11). For him to receive the name above every name, it was necessary that he not only die but that he also conquer death and thus gain a great victory over the devil (Heb. 2:14). There was only one way to do that.

Death and Resurrection

For all the wonderful truths concerning Christ's life and death, they are actually all falsehoods if the resurrection did not take place. The cross is incomplete without the resurrection, and vice versa. As J. Gresham Machen says, "The great weapon with which the disciples of Jesus set out to conquer the world was not a mere comprehension of eternal principles; it was a historical message, an account of something that had recently happened, it was the message, 'He is risen.'"[2] Paul speaks of the matters of "first importance":

> For I delivered to you as of first importance what I also received: that Christ died for our sins in accordance with the Scriptures, that he was buried, that he was raised on the third day in accordance with the Scriptures, and that he appeared to Cephas, then to the twelve. (1 Cor. 15:3–5)

The significance of Christ's resurrection is determined by the peculiar nature of his substitutionary death. The resurrection, then, must be interpreted in light of his death. He died to conquer the guilt and power of sin. Having been raised from the dead, Christ now sets about making this a reality in the lives of those for whom he died. The mere fact of his resurrection makes the promise of the forgiveness of sins so powerful in our lives.

Historical Context

As the Gospel narratives inform us, the Pharisees believed in the resurrection, but the Sadducees did not. Outside Jewish thought, some Greek philosophers believed in life after death, but this was a sort of disembodied immortality. Quite unlike anyone else before them, the early Christians believed in the resurrection of the dead in terms of bodily form. Many of these Christians came from pagan backgrounds and would have previously thought that such a thing was silly.

The early Christians did, in fact, deviate from typical Jewish belief in the resurrection in some respects. Most important, the Christians believed that the resurrection had actually happened to one person in a unique way that was, in a sense, the "firstfruits" of every other person who would be raised to eternal life in the body (1 Cor. 15:20). Thus, the resurrection of Jesus and our resurrection cannot be separated, though they are distinct. As the "firstfruits," Christ's resurrection is the part of the whole; he is the "firstborn from the dead" (Col. 1:18). This was the "innovation" of Christianity: bringing the future into the present.

Because the body of Jesus in the tomb was not destroyed but rather transformed, Christians also believe in the resurrection in terms of *transformation*. Some resurrection-believing Jewish people in the first century had ideas about the future body, but they thought it would be either basically the same as our current body or some sort of luminous body, starlike in its appearance. But Paul has in mind a sort of glorified body that is no longer susceptible to pain and suffering (better than what we have) but still truly human (not "starlike").

The "crazy" claim of the Christians, and especially the apostles who preached publicly, was that Israel's Messiah had been raised from the dead: "This Jesus God raised up, and of that we all are witnesses. . . . Let all the house of Israel therefore know for certain that God has made him both Lord and Christ, this Jesus whom you crucified" (Acts 2:32, 36). This claim was viewed as crazy because, according to first-century Jews, Israel's messiah was not supposed to die. He was supposed to conquer the Romans and deliver Israel in such a way that Israel would usher in a new age that would see the Old Testament prophecies fulfilled in terms of Israel ruling in worldwide dominion.

But instead, Israel's Messiah died, and so did the hopes of Christ's followers, who by and large abandoned him. Yet the New Testament Epistles make it clear just how central the resurrection is to Christian belief and practice. Something must have happened to these writers so that they essentially based every bit of truth that they spoke of on the historical fact of the resurrection. If Christ was in fact raised, then everything mattered, and nothing was to be feared, since Christians are guaranteed glorious new bodies like the body of Christ (Phil. 3:21).

As for the Christian faith, you need to believe in the bodily resurrection of Christ and those who are necessarily joined to him. His resurrection happened in the first century; ours will happen in the future when he returns (1 John 3:2). If, however, Christ has not been raised from the dead, bodily, then our faith is in vain (1 Cor. 15:14). Our resurrection to life depends on his resurrection. Christianity without the resurrection of Christ is a worthless stench that deserves the ridicule and abandonment of all who profess the name Christian. But we do not have that choice because "*in fact* Christ has been raised from the dead, the firstfruits of those who have fallen asleep" (1 Cor. 15:20).

The Theological Significance

The resurrection does not only change everything for us in terms of our hope and destiny, but it also changed everything for Christ. In the beginning of Paul's letter to the Romans, he describes Jesus as the one "declared to be the Son of God in power according to the Spirit of holiness by his resurrection from the dead" (Rom. 1:4). Jesus is now exalted "in power."

He has moved from a state of humiliation (womb to tomb) to a state of exaltation (resurrection to enthronement).

Accordingly, as Paul says, we know that since the Father raised Jesus, he will also raise us with Jesus and bring us from our own state of "humiliation" to our eternal state of "exaltation" in the heavenly places (2 Cor. 4:14). How are we to attain to this glorious end? We are to confess with our mouths and believe in our hearts that God raised Jesus, Israel's Messiah, from the dead (Rom. 10:8–9).

As noted, whatever is true of Christ becomes true of his people. Christ was raised, which means Paul can describe the Colossians as "having been buried with him in baptism, in which you were also raised with him through faith in the powerful working of God, who raised him from the dead" (Col. 2:12). And he can instruct them, "If then you have been raised with Christ, seek the things that are above, where Christ is, seated at the right hand of God" (Col. 3:1).

What we have, especially resurrection life, is handed to us from Christ, who had to possess the blessing himself before we could; hence, he is "the head of the body, the church. He is the beginning, the firstborn from the dead, that in everything he might be preeminent" (Col. 1:18).

Jesus was justified so that we might be justified (Isa. 50:8; 1 Tim. 3:16). His resurrection was his public vindication, which led to further vindication when he ascended on high and poured out his Spirit (Rom. 8:9) on the church. We are justified because of Christ's obedience, death, and resurrection. God's declarative act of pronouncing us righteous depends on Christ's resurrection (Rom. 4:25; 1 Cor. 15:17). If Christ was made sin for his people, he therefore needed a public justification/vindication from his Father for his sinless life and victorious death. Condemnation at the cross was answered with vindication at the tomb. The resurrection proves that Jesus really was "the righteous one" (Isa. 53:10–11).

This means that our vindication is not in doubt. If Christ was vindicated, so shall we be. Since God raised Jesus from the dead, we have proof that Christ's satisfaction was accepted on our behalf. We were represented with Christ in his death and resurrection, of which baptism is a visible testimony of this truth (Rom. 6:1–11). And so, as you can see, Christ's resurrection grants us assurance but also provides us with the ground for our Christian piety: we have been raised with him and so ought to seek the things that are above (Col. 3:1).

Christ's Ascension and Heavenly Seat

Just as Christ's resurrection and death are joined as equally meaningful truths that depend on one another, we may also say that Christ's ascension is appropriately joined to his resurrection. Christ came to earth to do a lot of things. But when was the last time you heard that Jesus came to give a priestly benediction? It was the last thing Christ did on earth: "And he led them out as far as Bethany, and lifting up his hands he blessed them. While he blessed them, he parted from them and was carried up into heaven" (Luke 24:50–51).

We should not understate the importance of this priestly blessing from the lips of the prophet who is king over all: in blessing his people, he thus entitled them to all the spiritual blessings of heaven (Eph. 1:3–4). Moreover, this blessing signified to his apostles that the curse was gone and that fellowship had been restored. Christ's ascension after his death and resurrection represented a military triumph; he had defeated his enemies and was now distributing gifts to the church. That Christ blesses the church in Luke 24:50–51 shows that a new creation has been ushered in. Christ's blessing fulfills the first blessing given to Adam and Eve (Gen. 1:28), and Matthew 28:19 ("Go therefore and make disciples of all nations") fulfills the original creation mandate to "be fruitful and multiply." Christ's ascension inevitably leads him to heaven but not in any ordinary manner. As the victorious conqueror, Christ enters heaven to sit at the right hand of the Father, which shows that he has done his work and that his work of satisfaction is finished. In other words, he has moved definitively from his state of humiliation to his state of exaltation. His work continues but only as the exalted prophet, priest, and king who continually intercedes at the right hand of the Father.

Those who wish to be acquainted with the true faith that we profess to hold must meditate on Christ's entrance into heaven. Perhaps Psalm 24 was a fitting song for heaven to sing at the entrance of Christ:

> Lift up your heads, O gates!
> And be lifted up, O ancient doors,
> that the King of glory may come in.
> Who is this King of glory?
> The LORD, strong and mighty,
> the LORD, mighty in battle!
> Lift up your heads, O gates!
> And lift them up, O ancient doors,
> that the King of glory may come in.
> Who is this King of glory?
> The LORD of hosts,
> he is the King of glory! *Selah* (Ps. 24:7–10)

The opening of heaven to the "King of glory" was the reception of the glorified God-man. As John Owen wonderfully puts it,

No heart can conceive that ineffable addition of glory which they [i.e., the Old Testament saints] received hereby. The mystery of the wisdom and grace of God in their redemption and salvation by Christ was now fully represented unto them; what they had prayed for, longed for, and desired to see in the days of their flesh on the earth, and waited for so long in heaven, was now gloriously made manifest unto them. Hereon did glorious light and blessed satisfaction come into and upon all those blessed souls, who died in the faith, but had not received the promise,—only beheld it afar off. And hereby did God greatly manifest his own glory in them and unto them; which is the first end of the continuation of this state of things in heaven. *This makes me judge that the season of Christ's entrance into heaven, as the holy sanctuary of God, was the greatest instance of created glory that ever was or ever shall be, unto the consummation of all things.*[3]

Christianity is heavenly minded (and heaven anticipated) because that is where Christ is with those saints who have departed from the struggle of this world and now behold his glory in their own glorious estate (John 17:24). When Christ arrived in heaven as the triumphant conqueror of the devil, heaven had an added glory and will now forever be Christ's heaven. His ascension, after he blessed the church, should be a doctrine, I think, that we meditate on a great deal more than we do.

In Ephesians 1, toward the end of that glorious chapter, Paul again highlights that the Father raised Jesus from the dead and "seated him at his right hand in the heavenly places" (Eph. 1:20). In this position, Christ occupies "all rule and authority and power and dominion" now and forever (Eph. 1:21). God, being a spirit, has no right hand or left hand. But this metaphor highlights that Christ has been invested with, as Ephesians 1:21 says, all authority and power. The man Christ Jesus is seated in glory with angels and saints adoring and worshiping him. He sits not idly but rather actively, making sure that his power and authority are not wasted.

All that the human nature can receive by way of communications from the divine nature is fulfilled at the right hand of the Father. As Thomas Watson says, "Christ as mediator is filled with all majesty and honour, beyond the comprehension of the highest order of angels."[4] He adds,

> In his humiliation he descended so low, that it was not fit to go lower; and in his exaltation he ascended so high that it was not possible to go higher. In his resurrection he was exalted above the grave, in his ascension he was exalted above the airy and starry heavens, in his sitting at God's right hand he was exalted far above the highest heavens (Eph. 4:10).[5]

What I need to know as a Christian is this essential truth: that the one I serve and put my faith in is the one who lived in shame and died in shame but rose in glory and ascended in glory and now reigns in glory. And if I belong to him, then I have all I need and do not need anything else. This is Christianity, and it is a Christianity worth knowing, loving, and confessing.

8

Redemption Applied

An ancient proverb says, "That alone belongs to you which you have bestowed."[1] What Jesus bestows on us belongs to him. But as we will see, Jesus bestows his gifts in a unique manner, for what he gives he still retains, even though he is able to give to all indiscriminately.

In his *Institutes of the Christian Religion*, John Calvin asks, "How do we receive those benefits which the Father bestowed on his only begotten Son—not for Christ's own private use, but that he might enrich poor and needy men?" His answer is perhaps one of the most famous quotes to come from the pen of a theologian in the time of the Reformation: "First, we must understand that as long as Christ remains outside of us, and we are separated from him, all that he has suffered and done for the salvation of the human race remains useless and of no value for us."[2]

While it is true that we come to enjoy Christ through faith by the "secret energy of the Spirit,"[3] we must keep in mind that Christ himself has been given authority to bestow the Spirit in his name, and so all our salvation benefits come from his hand. What happens, in short, is this: the blessings we receive are all from Christ because these blessings are all true *of* Christ.

Union with Christ

Union with Christ is commonly spoken of in the New Testament with reference to believers by their being "in Christ" or "in him."[4] Usually Paul opens a letter using this designation for those who are saints; for example, in Ephesians 1:1, he states, "To the saints who are in Ephesus, and are faithful in Christ Jesus" (see also 1 Cor. 1:2; Phil. 1:1; Col. 1:2; 1 Thess. 1:1; 2 Thess. 1:1).

The gospel involves the Holy One of God joining himself to those who are unclean and making them spotless and without blemish through his union with his bride. Christ takes the initiative and joins himself to us through the secret working of the Spirit. But make no mistake: we do not simply have the Spirit dwelling in us, but we have the Spirit of Christ dwelling in us (Rom. 8:9), so that we may say, Christ dwells in our hearts through faith (Eph. 3:17).

I think the great Dutch theologian Herman Witsius speaks well on the dynamics of the spiritual union between the Lord Jesus and his bride:

> By a true and real union, (but which is only passive on their part,) [the elect] are united to Christ when his Spirit first takes possession of them, and infuses into them a principle of new life: the beginning of which life can be from nothing else but from union with the Spirit of Christ. . . . Further, since faith is an act flowing from the principle of spiritual life, it is plain, that in a sound sense, it may be said, an elect person is truly and really united to Christ before actual faith.[5]

The point that needs to be emphasized is rather simple but very important for how we conceive of salvation. Why do we believe? Some have battled long and hard, even in recent times, over whether regeneration precedes faith, or vice versa. But I want to state that the really important question is, When does Christ, by his Spirit, take possession of us? This is the crucial question that answers the others. Thomas Goodwin makes a similar observation. He calls union with Christ the "first fundamental thing of justification, and sanctification and all."[6] But more specifically, in relation to regeneration, we may say that union precedes regeneration. According to Goodwin, Christ first "apprehends" the believer: "It is not my being regenerate that puts me into a right of all those privileges, but it is Christ [who] takes me, and then gives me his Spirit, faith, holiness, etc."[7]

I emphasize this point to say that the prerogative of granting all the blessings obtained by Christ to us belongs to none other than Christ himself. He came to save sinners, and he makes sure that he will save sinners by uniting himself to them in order to secure them to himself forever. Based on his intercession for us, he receives the Spirit in order to personally bestow on us all that we can possibly receive from him, though the effect of some of the blessings we receive may be delayed according to their peculiar nature (e.g., our glorified bodies).

The gift of faith that we receive is a gift given to us from Christ himself; indeed, we are dead in our sins, and Christ joins himself to us and secretly grants gifts such as faith to us. The faith given to us is necessary insofar as the act of our will formally and publicly completes the union with Christ and the believer (i.e., "mutual union"). This means we are simply confirming the union that has happened when we respond in faith to the risen Savior. Christ's Spirit first apprehends us so that we might respond, by faith, and complete, in a public way (Rom. 10:8–9), the marriage relationship. We live by faith for Christ because he has made us his own (Phil. 3:12).

Faith

Faith—a supernatural gift from God, delivered to us through union with Christ, applied by the working of the Spirit—involves assent not simply to the truth that God has revealed but to the person of Christ. The principle by which we think and act in relation to God is by faith. We live, day to day, by faith. Faith involves our trust (Ps. 78:22). But faith recognizes Christ and the gospel as true, so that we cannot but give assent to the claims of the word of God. As B. B. Warfield says, "The conception embodied in the terms 'belief,' 'faith,' in other words, is not that of an arbitrary act of the subject's; it is that of a mental state or act which is determined by sufficient reasons."[8] Now if Christ grants us faith, he will not grant us a faith that isn't ultimately satisfied by anything less than Christ himself. That is, indeed, good news: to know that our faith cannot fail because it necessarily finds solace and fulfillment only in the one who gave us the gift in the first place.

The faith given to us may be in doctrines, in words, or in persons. Ultimately, faith leads to salvation because of its central focus: the person of Christ. Faith trusts in the "powerful working of God" (Col. 2:12). God put forward the person and work of Jesus to be received by faith (Rom. 3:25). Faith does not merely help us escape God's wrath (John 3:18), but it also brings us to God through Christ. It is not meant to act as a "get out of jail free" card but rather as a grace by which we look continually to our triune God, knowing that he is for us and in us.

We receive Christ by faith and abide in Christ by faith (John 1:12; 15:1–11). We trust God that his provision of Christ is the only suitable solution to our only real problems. Looking to Jesus is the looking that comes from faith (Heb. 12:2). There is a great deal to be said about faith, including the elements of knowledge, assent, and trust. But we cannot make the mistake of forgetting to say that Jesus grants us faith as his gift in order that we may look to him. That, I think, is the principal reason why we receive such a gift. True, we receive justification through faith and thus have peace with God. But what is the goal of our faith? Surely it is the principle by which we daily fix our eyes on Jesus. Faith is not a one-time act, merely for the purpose of getting us out of hell. Rather, the New Testament faith that is wondrously described in so many ways is the faith that receives, rests in, and focuses on the person of Christ.

Christianity for the believer is the life of faith so that we can say with the apostle Paul, "I have been crucified with Christ. It is no longer I who live, but Christ who lives in me. And the life I now live in the flesh I live by faith in the Son of God, who loved me and gave himself for me" (Gal. 2:20). Christ lives in us so that we may live in him and for him, because there is no other proper response to one who gave himself so freely and lovingly for our sakes.

The Christ-Focused Order of Salvation

John 1:16 testifies of Christ, "For from his fullness we have all received, grace upon grace." We may be rightly tempted to focus in this verse on what it means to receive grace upon (or instead of) grace, but we must not miss the fact that we receive grace from Christ's fullness. This is a tricky concept, sometimes glossed over or misunderstood to mean "from Christ's divinity we receive grace." But I think there is a more compelling argument to be made regarding this verse and how it relates to all the blessings we receive from Christ.

When we speak about the so-called order of salvation, we are talking about the way and manner in which we receive such blessings as justification, adoption, and sanctification. Of course, these blessings are a result of the union with Christ that we have in eternity. Romans 8:28–30, for all the debate surrounding it, is actually quite clear in its meaning:

> And we know that for those who love God all things work together for good, for those who are called according to his purpose. For those whom he foreknew he also predestined to be conformed to the image of his Son, in order that he might be the firstborn among many brothers. And those whom he predestined he also called, and those whom he called he also justified, and those whom he justified he also glorified.

This passage has been famously called "the golden chain of salvation," owing to the influence of the father of English Puritanism, William Perkins. The blessings offered in this "chain" are distinct but not separate. They form an unbreakable bond, so that those who are predestined will necessarily be called, justified, and glorified. It is not hard to show in Paul's writings that "glorified" is a sort of "already–not yet" term that can easily include the doctrine of sanctification (see 2 Cor. 3:18).

But clearly there is a focus not just on the blessings but also on the purposes of God. He predestines us to be "conformed to the image of his Son" (Rom. 8:29) so that Christ may be the preeminent one in all things. Calvin was often concerned to retain the words *in Christ* rather than *by Christ* because "once we are made one with him, he shares with us all that he has received from the Father."[9] Union with Christ is the heartbeat of the Christian life.

As I have said, we participate in Christ's death and resurrection because he represents our interests as one of us, and thus he is our substitutionary mediator (Rom. 6:5–11; Col. 2:9–15). The fruits of his resurrection victory are ours. We have passed from wrath to grace because Jesus himself passed from wrath (Matt. 27:46, "My God, my God, why have you forsaken me?") to grace (Rom. 1:4, "and was declared to be the Son of God in power according to the Spirit of holiness by his resurrection from the dead, Jesus Christ our Lord").

Regeneration is the beginning of new life in us when the Spirit overshadows us and falls on us and in us, which is representative of the "new beginning" of Christ's life in the womb of the virgin: "And the angel answered her, 'The Holy Spirit will come upon you, and the power of the Most High will overshadow you; therefore the child to be born will be called holy— the Son of God'" (Luke 1:35). The Spirit gives us new life, just as he gave Jesus "new life" (i.e., his human nature).

In terms of our justification before God, we need to see it as rooted in Christ's own justification. Hence, Christ's justification is his resurrection: "He was manifested in the flesh, *vindicated* by the Spirit" (1 Tim. 3:16). God declared his Son righteous, and he vindicated (justified) him publicly; by faith alone we are declared righteous, and God will one day publicly vindicate us.

Adoption is also a gift given from Christ because it is true of Christ. The eternal Son became flesh, and in that state he was also the son of a woman (Mary) and was adopted to be the son of a man (Joseph). In the way that Hebrews 1 uses Psalm 2:7 and 2 Samuel 7:14, we see that Christ is declared to be God's

Son, the true king (Rom. 1:4). These are references to Christ's sonship as mediator, which highlight his office as king. The Father adopts Jesus as the man of the new age. Our union with Christ thus gives us a right to the title of sonship: Jesus is "the firstborn among many brothers" (Rom. 8:29).

From where do we get our holiness? Or, better, from whom do we get our holiness? We receive the holiness of Christ not only by imputation but also by impartation. Abraham Kuyper rightly says, "What a redeemed soul needs is human holiness."[10] The Spirit who was Christ's inseparable companion on earth stamps Christ's holiness on us as we are conformed to his image from one degree of glory to another. As Sinclair Ferguson says concerning the Spirit,

> Because of his ministry in Christ he can now indwell us to reproduce the same holiness in our lives. And so, adds Kuyper, "The Holy Spirit finds this holy disposition in its required form, not in the Father, nor in Himself, but in Immanuel, who as the Son of God and the Son of man possesses holiness in that peculiar form."[11]

What Christ was ignorant of in his ministry (Mark 13:32) he was no longer ignorant of because of his new state of exalted glory. Christ was under the dominion of sin at his death, but his resurrection broke that power forever. This conquest establishes the ground for our own conquest over sin's dominion in our lives (i.e., sanctification).

As mentioned above, Paul's use of "glorified" in Romans 8:30 likely includes sanctification. But glorification is more than just sanctification. Christ was glorified (John 17:1–5; 1 Cor. 15:45–49) to the point that he became a "life-giving Spirit" (1 Cor. 15:45, my trans.)—and, I believe, "Spirit" should be capitalized in this instance (contra ESV, NIV; cf. Rom. 8:9; 2 Cor. 3:17; 1 Pet. 1:11).

So when we are speaking about "redemption applied," I believe that we need to make sure that our thoughts gravitate toward Jesus. He unites himself to us, by a secret operation of his Spirit, and works many operations in our souls, including granting to us faith so that we can formally "tie the wedding knot" and be accounted as those who possess every spiritual blessing in Christ. Without our act of faith, we cannot claim to be Christians. What's more, the blessings we receive come not just by some divine fiat, whereby the Father says we are justified, adopted, sanctified, and glorified, but rather, we receive blessings that are true of Christ himself (but suited to our condition as sinners).

In other words, "That alone belongs to you which you have bestowed."

PART 3

THE
SPIRIT-ENERGIZED
LIFE

9

Gift

The Roman philosopher Seneca, who lived during the time of Christ, said, "While you look at what is given, look also at the giver."[1] When we look to the gift of the Son, we are immediately drawn to the giver of that gift: the Father (Rom. 8:32). As we look to the gift of the Holy Spirit, we need to be drawn to the giver of that gift: the Son. Looking to the Father and the Son should cause us to look to the Spirit and the importance of his person and work in our lives, not just in this life but also in the life to come.

Speaking in the seventeenth century, Thomas Goodwin once noted, "There is a general omission in the saints of God, in their not giving the Holy Ghost that glory that is due to his person. . . . The work he does for us in its kinds is as great as those of the Father or the Son."[2] I wonder if this is still true today for many of us. Do we live in awareness of our utter dependence on the Holy Spirit for our salvation? I am convinced that the church needs to develop a greater sense of the Spirit's work in our lives and specifically of the fact that the Christian faith and life from start to finish must be a Spirit-energized life.

The Holy Spirit is what theologians have called the second principle of gospel truth that reveals the glory of God. "For," says John Owen, "when God designed the great and glorious work of recovering fallen man and the saving of sinners . . . he appointed, in his infinite wisdom, two great means thereof. The one was *the giving of his Son for them*, and the other was *the giving of his Spirit unto them*."[3]

God the Father gave these two principal gifts to mankind. Indeed, nothing the Father had designed and purposed and nothing the Son had procured and purchased would have been of any benefit to us if the Spirit had not applied the works of the Father and the Son to us by his powerful, energetic, and mysterious work. The person and work of Jesus give meaning and purpose to the person and work of the Spirit on behalf of sinners, which manifests the very heart of Christianity.

Christ's Presence

The Holy Spirit as revealed in Scripture is energetic and active, full of life, and powerful in his work. Those who receive him cannot help but possess power, sometimes in the form of incredible gifts and abilities that can lead to creation, destruction, or renovation. The Spirit's work is multifaceted, done according to his purposes in creation and redemption.

Jesus was, as we have seen, the man of the Spirit *par excellence* during his ministry on earth. But there is a sense in which the Spirit was—as appointed by the Father—Christ's "lord." Hence the Spirit drives Christ into the wilderness (Mark 1:12). But it appears that while Christ was in a state of submission to the Spirit during his state of humiliation, upon his entrance into the state of exaltation, he entered into a new relation toward the Spirit (i.e., one of power and lordship). In the last phrase from 2 Corinthians 3:18, there are a few possible translations: "from the Lord, who is the Spirit" (NIV); "from the Lord, the Spirit" (NASB); "from the Lord who is the Spirit" (ESV). But we could also render the Greek as "from the Lord of the Spirit," which is actually a very natural translation of the Greek and yields an important theological observation concerning the relationship between Christ and the Spirit. As Sinclair Ferguson, who prefers the last rendering, notes in his excellent book on the Holy Spirit, "Paul is saying that the Lord Jesus Christ is Lord of the Spirit. There is no ontological confusion here, but an economic equivalence; nor is there an ontological subordinationism, but rather a complete intimacy of relationship between Jesus and the Spirit."[4] The Spirit proceeds from the Father and the Son, ontologically speaking. But note, there is a beautiful analogy in the sense that the resurrected Lord sends forth the Spirit in his name (i.e., the Spirit of Christ) so that the character and life of Jesus may be imprinted on his people.[5]

At the heart of certain momentous shifts in God's dealings with humanity emerges the special work of the Holy Spirit. As Christ in his person and work comes into clearer view, so does the Spirit. There is a necessary relation between the gradual unfolding of revelation concerning the person and work of Christ and thus also concerning the person and work of the Holy Spirit. To understand one person, you must understand the other.

In between his resurrection and ascension, Jesus taught and gave commands "through the Holy Spirit to the apostles whom he had chosen" (Acts 1:2). He also made a promise shortly thereafter: "You heard from me; for John baptized with water, but you will be baptized with the Holy Spirit not many days from now" (Acts 1:4–5).

How did Jesus know beforehand what would happen regarding the coming of the Spirit? His Upper Room Discourse provides enough explicit testimony for us to understand that Jesus was (and is) in full control of the church. Knowing the importance of his public ministry in the flesh, with the whole world watching, Jesus, nevertheless, was able to tell his disciples that it was to their advantage that he leave them; otherwise, the Helper (i.e., the Spirit) would not come to them. Christ would send the Helper to them (John 16:7). Jesus is the giver of the Spirit.

How could it be to the advantage of the disciples for Jesus to leave? In this way: the very Spirit who empowered Christ during his ministry was the same Spirit who would empower Christ's disciples in their ministry and Christians today in our various callings. But there emerges a marvel of the new covenant era, in which Christ returns to heaven as the God-man, the one who has conquered the devil. Jesus may have left bodily, but he is still present with his disciples by way of the Spirit, the very Spirit of Christ (or "Spirit of Jesus," Acts 16:7). The Helper who comes to us comes in the name and for the sake of Jesus.

Jesus left to go to his Father, but he is still present, remarkably, because he sends the Spirit from the Father to bear witness to his person and work for the building up of his bride. He truly is with his people and knows it. In the Great Commission to his disciples, he gives the comforting words that he will be with them "always, to the end of the age" (Matt. 28:20). If he has left them bodily, then by this statement, he can only mean that he is with them by the powerful indwelling presence of the Spirit. To have the Spirit is to have Christ. To not possess the Spirit is to not possess Christ (Rom. 8:9).

The risen Lord is a life-giving Spirit (1 Cor. 15:45). He gives life and power because he gives the Spirit. The Spirit in turn brings glory to Christ as his chief work on earth: "He [the Spirit] will glorify me, for he will take what is mine and declare it to you" (John 16:14). In one sense, we await the bodily return of Christ when he will come to judge the living and the dead. But in another sense, Christ is still with us because the Spirit indwells us, so that Christ dwells in our hearts through faith (Eph. 3:17). Thus, in the context of announcing his departure and the Spirit's coming, Jesus says, "I will not leave you as orphans; I will come to you" (John 14:18). This declaration is best understood not in terms of his postresurrection appearances or his second coming but in terms of his coming to his disciples by way of the Spirit.

Christianity foundationally involves understanding the person and work of the Spirit, especially in the new covenant era— though he was at work in the saints of the Old Testament—in a decidedly Christ-centered manner. As a term, *Christ-centered* can be and is abused; what I mean is simply this: that we need to ask what our doctrine of the Spirit has to do with the person of Christ at every turn in our theological thinking on the Spirit's ministry to the church today. A failure to do this can lead to disastrous consequences in our understanding of the Spirit's work.

Bestowal of Salvation[6]

Whatever saving good is given to us was first purposed by the Father, then purchased by the Son, and finally applied by the Spirit. We are not properly saved until that moment when the Spirit grants us spiritual life from heaven.

Jesus does not leave a new birth from heaven as optional for a potential believer. As Nicodemus found out, "Unless one is born again he cannot see the kingdom of God" (John 3:3). Many theologians have spoken of the doctrine of regeneration, which can mean either the whole process of spiritual life imparted to the believer or the initial "quickening" of a person from spiritual death to life. But we must be careful not to make regeneration a doctrine purely concerned with what happens to individuals. The regeneration of the saints testifies to God's renewal of all things, the dawning of a new age. The last Adam is giving life, and he will set about to renew all things one day. The regeneration by which we are given new life is linked to the renewal of all things and to God's ultimate resolve to one day re-create this world (2 Pet. 3:13).

Ultimately, everything the Father purposed, and especially what Christ did for the sake of his bride, is only of any value when the Spirit fulfills God's promises. William Whately (1583–1639) made this important point: "If Christ should come, and die, for one man, ten thousand times; all those deaths should profit that one man nothing at all for his salvation, unless he be made a new creature."[7] The truth is, however, that Christ will not die for someone with such an act of love and yet withhold another equally important act of love: the making alive of the person to receive the benefit of the cross.

Jesus comes into the world, having received a people given to him by the Father, and lays down his life for his sheep. He knows his sheep by name (John 10:14–15). It seems inconceivable to me that Jesus would show the greatest extent of his love to a person by dying for his or her sins on the cross but then withhold from that person the one thing that completes the purpose of his death, namely, the Spirit.

The principle of spiritual life that comes from above, from Christ, and descends on us and in us is the same principle of spiritual life that enables us to do that which is holy and acceptable to God. Jesus tells his disciples that apart from him we can do nothing, which is akin to saying that without the Spirit we can do nothing (John 15:5).

The Christian faith cannot leave open to debate the question whether we play any role in bringing ourselves from death to life. Most who call themselves evangelical Christians admit that we have been impaired by sin and that we need grace. For many, however, while grace may "excite" the will, the final hinge on which regeneration swings is our own will. In truth, regeneration must not be viewed as the cooperative act of man any more than lowering a coffin into the grave is the cooperative work of the person in it.

The Bible makes it clear that man is not merely impaired but is dead in trespasses and sins (Eph. 2:1–3). Regeneration involves a new heart and a new spirit—the natural man, being spiritually dead, cannot produce this new birth in himself. Petrus van Mastricht says, "If man were, either in whole or in part, the author of his own regeneration, he would enable himself to differ, contrary to the apostle's assertion [that we have nothing except what we have received] (1 Cor. 4:7)."[8] Man is passive in regeneration; he is born of the Spirit (John 3:5–6), born of God, and not born of anything in man, not his blood, his flesh, or his will (John 1:13).

The Spirit of God is the "efficient" cause, or the sole author, of regeneration. In this work we have no part. The believer can concur with the Spirit in his sanctification, says John Flavel (1628–1691), "but in the first production of this spiritual principle he can do nothing." Furthermore, if human nature could concur in regeneration, then "the best natures would be soonest quickened," but we more often see the worst of men regenerated.[9] In regeneration, humanity does not contribute to this work, because it is the sovereign and supernatural work of

God. The Spirit is the "efficient principle of it." In saying this, in regeneration divine grace reigns, and human nature is passive. Grace works on nature to give it life; nature cannot and does not cooperate with the new birth from above.

Once the Spirit makes us alive, we possess Christ and all that he has done for us. More remains to be applied to us, but we cannot receive anything better than what we first receive, because we first receive the triune God into our souls. As Augustus Toplady's hymn "A Debtor to Mercy Alone" so wonderfully states,

> My name from the palms of His hands
> Eternity will not erase;
> Imprest on His heart, it remains
> In marks of indelible grace.
> Yes! I to the end shall endure,
> As sure as the earnest is giv'n;
> *More happy, but not more secure,*
> When all earthly ties have been riv'n.[10]

Yes, the departed saints are more happy, but they are not more secure. The Spirit given to us is as great as the gift of the Son, since without either, we would not be redeemed.

10

Conviction

John Calvin opened his *Institutes of the Christian Religion* with these (now famous) words: "Nearly all the wisdom we possess, that is to say, true and sound wisdom, consists of two parts: the knowledge of God and of ourselves."[1] Knowledge of God is dangerous business for us humans but nevertheless essential. A true view of God, granted to us by the Spirit, will result in self-abnegation. This happened to godly Job toward the end of his trial:

> I had heard of you by the hearing of the ear,
>> but now my eye sees you;
> therefore I despise myself,
>> and repent in dust and ashes. (Job 42:5–6)

Those in the flesh need true self-awareness as well as awareness of God. Both of these are impossible to come by unless the Holy Spirit does his work, which is partly "negative" and partly "positive." Awareness of sin, conviction of sin, and repentance are glued together by the work of the Spirit, who, in God's purposes, leads sinners to Christ by making them aware that they need a Savior.

Sin

Ralph Venning provocatively remarked, "Sin is worse than Hell. . . . There is more evil in it, than good in all the Creation."[2] It is costly but free, demanding but easy, fun but miserable, corporate but personal. It has ruined countless lives and will ruin many more. Sin has temporal and eternal consequences. The world today, despite the advance of God's kingdom, is still a very bad place.

Of course, this was not so in the beginning. In the garden of Eden, after the creation of man and woman, God "saw everything that he had made, and behold, it was very good" (Gen. 1:31). Things were "good" before woman but "very good" afterward! In Eden, Adam and Eve had the moral law written in their hearts, and God gave them the ability to fulfill it. God had many intentions for them, no doubt, but who can deny that his goal for them was that they might glorify his name on earth through obedience to his commands? God never gave up this goal for mankind.

J. I. Packer once described the Puritan view of sin, which is both accurate and biblical, by noting that they "saw sin as a perverted energy within people that enslaves them to God-defying, self-gratifying behavior, and by distraction, deceit, and direct opposition weakens and overthrows their purposes of righteousness."[3]

There is much to say about sin—where it came from, how it is dealt with, and so on. But first we must understand that sin is rebellion against God. Most important, sin is hatred toward God. Sin is idolatrous (Rom. 1:25) and manifests itself in hostility toward God (Rom. 8:7). Fellow image bearers suffer from sin's consequences as well. Hostility toward God leads to hostility toward our fellow man (Rom. 1:26–31; Gal. 5:19–21). We know what sin is because God has given us his law, in both what it forbids and what it commands (Ex. 20:1–17; Eph. 4:17–32). The moral law remains binding on Christians in the new covenant era; otherwise, Romans 13:9–10 makes very little sense, as it declares, "For the commandments, 'You shall not commit adultery, You shall not murder, You shall not steal, You shall not covet,' and any other commandment, are summed up in this word: 'You shall love your neighbor as yourself.'"

No one has gone personally unaffected by the contagion of sin (Ps. 51:5). It is truly universal (Rom. 3:23), so that the gospel functions as a universal remedy. Ministers always have a message for every person because of the universality of sin. It would be hard to understand why everyone sins unless we were all born in sin. But because sin came from Adam to all men, because all sinned, all who die testify loudly to creation that they are in fact sinners (see Rom. 5:12–19). Denying that we are guilty in Adam but affirming that we inherited sin from Adam, as some theologians do, is surely a distinction without a difference in the end.[4]

Sin enslaves us and keeps us busy. The depravity of our natures, apart from redeeming grace, is extensive, affecting our bodies and souls, minds and wills, and so on. Those who sin are slaves to sin; they are those who are dead in their trespasses and sins (Eph. 2:1, 5). Sinners outside the kingdom are children of the devil who do his deeds and are, as such, children of wrath (Eph. 2:3).

Sin is so bad that when someone truly good comes into the world, the world kills such a person. People would rather have a murderer turned loose on them than have anything more to do with the Prince of Peace (Matt. 27:26).

The only hope for sinners is for them to know that they are sinners. We should know that we are sinners in a way that accurately reflects what God has told us about how we are sinners: in both a personal and a corporate manner.

Conviction of Sin

Conviction of sin has lost its rightful place in Christian thinking, piety, and preaching today. We no longer refer to people as God fearers anymore, and we do not speak as though being convicted of our sin is a good thing. Note Paul's description of public worship:

> But if all prophesy, and an unbeliever or outsider enters, he is convicted by all, he is called to account by all, the secrets of his heart are disclosed, and so, falling on his face, he will worship God and declare that God is really among you. (1 Cor. 14:24–25)

True conviction, through the public declaration of God's word, leads to worship. Those convicted by the Spirit are led to rejoice in God's provision for sinners:

> Fools mock at the guilt offering,
>   but the upright enjoy acceptance. (Prov. 14:9)

To be convicted of sin by the Spirit is a gift of Christ to the church.

In John 16:8–11 Jesus speaks about the specific role of the Spirit (i.e., convicting of guilt) in relation to a host of interrelated issues:

> And when [the Spirit] comes, he will convict the world concerning sin and righteousness and judgment: concerning sin, because they do not believe in me; concerning righteousness, because I go to the Father, and you will see

me no longer; concerning judgment, because the ruler of this world is judged.

The verb translated "convict" here occurs in the New Testament with a great deal of frequency (e.g., Matt. 18:15; Luke 3:19; John 3:20; 8:46; 1 Cor. 14:24; Eph. 5:11, 13; 1 Tim. 5:20; 2 Tim. 4:2; Titus 1:9, 13; 2:15; Heb. 12:5; James 2:9; Jude 15, 22; Rev. 3:19). When this verb is used, it invariably involves someone being shown his or her sin.

If we keep in mind the close bond between the Son and the Spirit in the application of their work, we can understand perhaps what Christ is saying about the Spirit's work in the world. Just as Jesus brought division into the world, because he testified that the world's works were evil, the Holy Spirit will continue to do the work of Jesus in the same way. Since the Spirit bears witness about Jesus (John 15:26–27), his ministry will necessarily involve a division.

The world needs conviction regarding not only sin but also the world's view of righteousness and judgment. Unbelief, as we have seen, is the worst and most damning sin. To bring a sinner out of a state of wrath and into a state of grace requires that the Spirit not only convict such a person of unbelief but also grant to the sinner the gift of faith to rectify this problem.

The world's righteousness is always in need of correcting. Religious "righteousness" and nonreligious righteousness require exposing (see Rom. 10:3; Phil. 3:6–9; Titus 3:5). Jesus exposed pretend righteousness while he was on earth (Matt. 23), and he continues this work through his Spirit. Those who follow Jesus, who live in the power of the Spirit and understand God's law, are tasked with speaking or preaching in a way that the Spirit will honor Christ and his word and bring conviction to those who possess only a pretended righteousness.

Many in the world argue that a woman has absolute rights over her own body, even if that means killing a baby in her womb, and they say that this is a good thing—a righteous thing. Thus, with such a pretended righteousness, the world judges in a manner that is morally wicked. Sometimes the people of God end up very much like the world. As Isaiah says,

> Woe to those who call evil good
> > and good evil,
> who put darkness for light
> > and light for darkness. (Isa. 5:20)

Whether the Roman Catholic Church with its laws on celibacy or countries with abortion "rights" that amount to murder, the world very much suffers from many judgments that are just plain wrong. False judgment can be tied to Satan, who was a liar from the beginning (John 8:42–47). The Spirit exposes false judgments and lies; he exposes false righteousness; and he brings conviction of sin to those who, apart from his work, naturally remain in a state of being filled with the mock righteousness and erroneous judgment that can lead only to condemnation.

Repentance

Repentance is a major theme throughout the Scriptures and so rightly forms a major part of the Christian faith. The Old Testament has a few words and phrases that highlight the nature of repentance, especially *nakham* and *shub*. The former has in view sorrow or regret; the latter means "to return." The beauty of repentance is illustrated in Psalm 51, where David ransacks the biblical vocabulary for sin as well as grace. The bridge between sin and grace is repentance. Repentance leads to life:

But if a wicked person turns away from all his sins that he has committed and keeps all my statutes and does what is just and right, he shall surely live; he shall not die. None of the transgressions that he has committed shall be remembered against him; for the righteousness that he has done he shall live. (Ezek. 18:21–22)

In the New Testament, "repentance" (Gk. *metanoia*) is also a returning to God at the beginning of the Christian life, and this turning to God does not end until we die. As Luther said in the first of his Ninety-Five Theses, "When our Lord and Master Jesus Christ said, 'Repent' (Mt 4:17), he willed the entire life of believers to be one of repentance."[5] To repent is not merely to regret but to change direction. The Westminster Shorter Catechism (q. 87) offers one of the finest summaries of biblical repentance ever written:

Q: What is repentance unto life?
A: Repentance unto life is a saving grace (Acts 11:18), whereby a sinner, out of a true sense of his sin (Acts 2:37–38), and apprehension of the mercy of God in Christ (Joel 2:13), doth, with grief and hatred of his sin, turn from it unto God (Jer. 31:18–19), with full purpose of, and endeavor after, new obedience (2 Cor. 7:11; Ps. 119:59).

Since repentance is a saving grace, we cannot exercise true repentance unless the Spirit grants it to us. It is not enough to feel bad that we have sinned; we must turn to God and seek to live in a way that is different from the pattern of sin we have repented from.

Because repentance issues forth from faith and looks to the mercy of God in Christ, we may call repentance "a second innocence." To be good is to acknowledge that we have been bad. The seventeenth-century poet John Milton calls repentance "that golden key that opens the palace of eternity."[6] He is right. There is no going to heaven without, on the road, repenting for what, apart from grace, makes us unfit for heaven.

In various Puritan writings—where, apparently, they were quoting the early church father Origen—we read of repentance as "the vomit of the soul."[7] We are inwardly humbled, we vomit out to God our confessions of sin, and we outwardly produce "fruit in keeping with repentance" (Matt. 3:8). If the Spirit is not active in these acts, then these acts are, ultimately, not a waste of time but rather actually impossible to do. By the Spirit we put to death the misdeeds of the flesh (Rom. 8:13), which includes the constant acts of repentance that accompany the process of being conformed to the image of the man of the Spirit, Jesus Christ.

There is also a sense in which repentance can be corporate, but these are tricky waters to navigate. An example comes from 2 Corinthians 7:8–11. Paul had written to the Corinthians and had grieved them into repenting, which was a "godly grief" (7:9). This made Paul rejoice. Why? This type of repentance leads to salvation, compared with the worldly grief that leads to death (7:10). Paul even highlights some of the core features of true repentance in the living example of the Corinthians: "For see what earnestness this godly grief has produced in you, but also what eagerness to clear yourselves, what indignation, what fear, what longing, what zeal, what punishment [i.e., justice]! At every point you have proved yourselves innocent in the matter" (7:11).

While we cannot be certain as to exactly what all these fruits mean, Paul clearly has a positive view of Christian graces such as eagerness, zeal, and fear, which are all tied to repentance. Sometimes a church or a group of people in a church will need to repent corporately for a specific sin. For example, one would think that the church of Laodicea needed to repent for their lukewarm attitude and materialistic pride (Rev. 3:14–21).

In the end, if we want to come to Christ, have fellowship with him, and enter through the narrow gate that leads to life, we will need to experience the Spirit-wrought graces of conviction and repentance. We cannot have Christ on our own terms; we must be his on his terms. And the Spirit is the person who brings us to Christ as those who renounce self-righteousness, receive Christ's perfect righteousness, and aim to live righteously by hating and forsaking our sins.

Any form of Christianity that glosses over the core doctrines of sin and repentance is not the pure, undiluted Christianity of the Scriptures. Christianity cannot stand with the legs of human self-righteousness carrying the infinite weight of sin. Only Christ, the God-man, can withstand the pressure of such a weight. He sends his Spirit to make sure we understand that truth in our frequent confessions of our unworthiness before God.

11

Holiness

Bishop J. C. Ryle astutely observes,

> A man may go to great lengths, and yet never reach true holiness. It is not knowledge—Balaam had that; nor great profession—Judas Iscariot had that; nor doing lots of things—Herod did that; nor zeal for certain matters in religion—Jehu had that; nor morality and outward respectability of conduct—the rich young ruler had that; nor taking pleasure in hearing preachers—the Jews in Ezekiel's time had that; nor keeping company with godly people—Joab and Gehazi and Demas had that. Yet none of these was holy! These things alone are not holiness. A man or woman may have any one of them, and yet never see the Lord.[1]

Holiness is possible only when the Holy Spirit works spiritual life in us (Gal. 5:22). His goal is truly Christ focused. He wants to transform us into the likeness of Christ. "Christiformity" is his principal work in sinners on earth; in fact, God's purpose in electing us is for the same end: "For those whom he foreknew he also predestined to be conformed to the image of his Son, in order that he might be the firstborn among many brothers" (Rom. 8:29). Adam and Eve were made in the image of God (Gen. 1:26–27), but sin entered the world and defaced God's image in us. The Father, Son, and Holy Spirit all share in the same purpose, that redeemed image bearers should reflect Christ, the visible image of the invisible God (Col. 1:15).

Holiness in Relation to Justification

Martin Luther, whom some wrongly think was weak on holiness, said in his commentary on Galatians,

> We conclude therefore with Paul, "that we are justified by faith only in Christ, without the law." Now after that a man is once justified, and possesses Christ by faith, and knows that he is his righteousness and life, doubtless he will not be idle, but as a good tree he will bring forth good fruits. For the believing man has the Holy Ghost; and where the Holy Ghost dwells, He will not suffer a man to be idle, but stirs him up to all exercises of piety and Godliness, and of true religion, to the love of God, to the patient suffering of afflictions, to prayer, to thanksgiving, to the exercise of charity towards all men.[2]

Martin Luther was, of course, right. There is a certain logical order in the Christian life whereby we are justified by faith and therefore bring forth fruit in keeping with holiness. Make no mistake: the order is important. We are not holy in order to be justified. We are justified, and then the process of sanctification takes place, which involves a lifelong battle with indwelling sin. But the battle against sin is fruitless if there has not been a declaration of pardon from Almighty God.

The apostle Paul wrote to the Corinthians, "For I delivered to you as of first importance what I also received: that Christ died for our sins in accordance with the Scriptures" (1 Cor. 15:3). One aspect of this good news is the glorious Christian doctrine of forgiveness of sins. As we confess in the Apostles' Creed, "I believe in . . . the forgiveness of sins." God washes away our sins, and this gives us assurance that we not only have eternal life but are also his children, who need not fear his condemnation. The Spirit seals to our hearts this glorious truth so that we can live in freedom and not bondage. This is an essential part of our sanctification.

But what makes our justification "doubly glorious" is the other side of the coin: that through faith in Jesus Christ, we receive his righteousness so that when we stand before God at the judgment seat of Christ, we are as secure before God as Christ is himself. Why? We possess his righteousness by imputation through our union with Christ. As such, his righteousness really is ours, so that God's declaration of us as righteous is true.

One of the obvious examples of justification by imputation in the Scriptures is Abraham: "And [Abraham] believed the LORD, and he counted it to him as righteousness" (Gen. 15:6). Paul comments, "But the words 'it was counted to him' were not written for his sake alone, but for ours also. It will be counted to us who believe in him who raised from the dead Jesus our Lord" (Rom. 4:23–24). As Abraham was justified by faith, so all others who wish to be saved must be justified by faith. Our justification consists not only in the nonimputation of our sin but also in the imputation ("crediting") of Christ's righteousness to us.

This doctrine has not always been popular or well understood in the church. Writing in the seventeenth century, John Owen said about the doctrine of imputation, "Yet is it so fallen out in our days, that nothing in religion is more maligned, more reproached, more despised, than the imputation of righteousness unto us, or an imputed righteousness."[3]

When discussing imputation, we aren't debating a doctrine that has little to do with Christian piety. Rather, this doctrine is at the heart of Christian assurance and peace with God. While Protestant theologians have defended imputation in different manners, in the main they have held basic agreement that

> we are not righteous before God by an inherent, but by an imputed righteousness, nor was Christ made sin by inherent, but imputed, guilt. The same way that his righteousness is communicated to us, our sin was communicated to him. Righteousness was inherent in him, but imputed to us; sin was inherent in us, but imputed to him.[4]

So, we may ask, what does justification by faith alone have to do with holiness? God does not justify a person without also granting to that person the gift of sanctification. As we live, we live confidently (but not presumptuously) before God because of what he has declared to be true of us: we are forgiven and possess, by way of imputation, the righteousness of another, namely, the Son of God, who is crowned with glory and honor. This is a truth that can be received, embraced, and cherished only because of the work of the Spirit.

Holiness

Over the course of the Christian church, few have ventured to deny the necessity of personal holiness in the life of a Christian. We might as well deny God's holiness if we are going to deny Christian holiness. After all, God's holy nature is the ground by which believers, whether in the Old or New Testaments, are called to be holy (Ex. 19:6; Lev. 11:44; 19:2; 20:7, 26; 21:8; 1 Pet. 1:16; 1 Thess. 4:7–8). How can there be communion between a (thrice) holy God and an unholy people?

But what is holiness? Holiness in the Scriptures has to do with drawing near to God because he has separated persons and things apart for a special purpose. There are degrees of holiness in the Old Testament. One has only to think of the events surrounding Mount Sinai (Ex. 3:5). Or consider that, compared to the (holy) Israelites, the high priest was most holy—he alone was able to enter the Most Holy Place (Heb. 9:7). This tells us that holiness is not, in the first place, about personal piety but about status.

This forms the background to the New Testament concept of the priesthood of all believers. The various gradations of holiness no longer exist. We all, as a body, enter the Most Holy Place, even those whose personal piety may not be as strong as that of the person sitting beside them in the pew. Hence, Paul writes to the Ephesians,

> Paul, an apostle of Christ Jesus by the will of God,
>
> To the saints who are in Ephesus, and are faithful in Christ Jesus. (Eph. 1:1)

He is essentially saying, "To those, who by God's grace, have been baptized and are now qualified as holy to enter the heavenly sanctuary (Heb. 12:18–24), peace be unto you."

God not only declares us to be justified, but he also declares us, positionally, to be saints (holy). The Spirit must honor that declaration, made by the Father for the sake of his Son. In fact, God refers to all his people as "holy" or as "saints," even beyond that simple declaration. So when the Spirit makes us alive in Christ, we experience a definitive and renovative break from the dominion of sin. Theologians speak of *definitive sanctification* as that which issues forth immediately from our union with Christ and makes us "new" creations and holy before God, those for whom, "in Christ, . . . the new has come" (2 Cor. 5:17). To be sure, we will progressively (more and more) yet imperfectly (in this life) die to sin and live to righteousness in the Christian life as we grow in holiness. Yet, rest assured, the Spirit has broken the bondage of sin for even the newest or weakest believers; all are truly regarded as holy ones of God—as saints. Importantly, this work of the Spirit keeps holiness (or sanctification) from being too individualistic and retains the proper biblical focus on the holy people of God. If God has declared us to be holy, he is also allowing us into his holy presence. We need our identity as "saints" in order to realize not only what is true about us but also what is expected of us as people designated by such a title.

The importance of holiness in God's people cannot be over-stated. Thomas Goodwin argues that it was God's "first aim that we should be holy before him."[5] He adds, "Though we be ordained to adoption and glory, yet we were first chosen to be 'holy before him in love.' . . . Without holiness here, there is no happiness to be expected hereafter. Without God's mercy we cannot be saved; and without holiness we are not under mercy (1 Peter 1:2)."[6] God is merciful toward us insofar as it is his aim to make us holy. To lack holiness is to lack God's mercy.

If we are going to plead for the necessity of holiness in the Christian life, there must be an encouraging motivation toward that end. The Christian faith insists on holiness but also provides the reasons for why we should be holy. It begins with our identity and status before a holy God. No doubt, we can never reciprocate the holiness that belongs exclusively to God (Job 4:18). This is why there must be a form of covenant condescension in the person of Christ. To be holy as God is holy means, surely, to be holy like his Son, Jesus Christ, who is the pattern and example of true holiness among humans.

Since we are "in Christ," God will accept a holiness from us that is not perfect, because he has already accepted us on the basis of Christ's perfect holiness, which is reckoned to our account. This is good news indeed. God knows we are but dust and ashes; he knows we are flesh; he is a gracious and compassionate God. So the holiness required of us as his people is a holiness that must be something we are capable of—it must be sincere, even if it is not perfect.

In Paul's letter to the Ephesians, he is not commanding them to do something utterly impossible when speaking of God's requirements for them. At the heart of his commands for holy living is the need for the saints in Ephesus to put off the old self and put on the new self, "created after the likeness of God in true righteousness and holiness" (Eph. 4:22–24). Holiness has a certain look, which is not simply about refraining from evil but also about doing the opposite. Those who used to lie must now speak the truth (4:25); those who used to steal should now work in order to be generous (4:28); and we should all be mindful not to "grieve the Holy Spirit of God" (4:30). But again, what is the motive for such behavior? Paul explains: "Be kind to one another, tenderhearted, forgiving one another, as God in Christ forgave you" (4:32). We live in a certain way—in obedience to God's moral law (Rom. 13:8–10)—because of how God has treated us in Christ and because we are now temples of the Spirit and should not wish to grieve him.

The Christian faith remains a positive one in the sense that our Christian living is defined not purely by what we do not do but also by what we do. "I do not play competitive sports on Sunday" should be balanced by "I get to worship with my brothers and sisters in the Lord and enjoy a day of rest." Keeping God's commandments is a positive endeavor for Christians. After all, in glory, we will think more of what we are doing than what we are not doing. So in this life, we must think as positively about holiness as we can: we live unto God in the name of Christ by the Spirit in obedience to his commandments.

Mortification

We sometimes speak of the work of the Spirit in our life in terms of his ability to move us to holiness: "His divine power has granted to us all things that pertain to life and godliness" (2 Pet. 1:3). This is important. But we should be clear, too, that there is an "ugly" side to holiness: death to sin and the death of sin. We are engaged in a holy war, with much plucking out and cutting off (Mark 9:43–48). The ultimate goal of holiness is complete conformity to Christ. This goal begins on earth, though it is consummated only when Christ returns (1 John 3:2).

Through union with Christ, we have died to sin (Rom. 6:2). If we have died to sin, how can we then sin? We belong to a new realm, whereby we have not only died to sin but also have been raised to new life—resurrection life. We do not sin, because we do not live in that former realm anymore. Remaining, or indwelling, sin is a reality for Christians, and we cannot deny that we still sin, for "if we say we have no sin, we deceive ourselves, and the truth is not in us" (1 John 1:8). The apostle John can affirm indwelling sin but also say, "No one born of God makes a practice of sinning, for God's seed abides in him; and he cannot keep on sinning, because he has been born of God" (1 John 3:9). Because the Holy Spirit dwells in us and works continually through the word, believers cannot live a life of continued willful sinning against God without denying who they are as newborn children of God. We practice righteousness, not sinning.

Paul speaks of this point rather forcefully in Romans 8:13: "For if you live according to the flesh you will die, but if by the Spirit you put to death the deeds of the body, you will live." He can offer this command because he has provided the necessary theological background, whether in Romans 3 or 6, for us to understand that killing sin, by the Spirit, is indeed possible and necessary. For example, in Romans 6:11–14, Paul teaches that the reign of sin has ended for Christians (6:11); that sin has lost its authority in our lives (6:12), which means we serve not sin but God (6:13); and that we can defeat sin because we live in an age of grace (6:14). Because of what has come before in Paul's letter, then, Romans 8:13 is not meant to be too shocking—even though it remains rather demanding.

The mortification of sin (i.e., "killing sin") is a duty that only believers, in the Spirit, can perform. As John Owen says in his penetrating work on mortification, "The choicest believers, who are assuredly freed from the condemning power of sin, ought yet to make it their business all their days to mortify the indwelling power of sin."[7] But the "principal efficient cause" (to use Owen's language) of mortification is by the power of the Spirit, given to us from Christ (John 15:5; Acts 2:33). The Spirit causes our hearts and minds to abound in grace so that the fruit of the Spirit in our lives is evident (Gal. 5:22). Our love is not love if it is not patient, kind, gentle, faithful, and so on. Why? The fruit of the Spirit means all his graces in us must be explained by each other. In other words, not only must we have both love and joy, but also our love must be joyous love. As we abound in these graces, we put to death those vices that are contrary to those of the Spirit (see Gal. 5:19–21).

Now the force of Paul's command in Romans 8:13 means that mortification, as an aspect of holy Christian living, is not an option (see Christ's words, too, in Matt. 5:29–30). If individuals do not mortify, they will die. But if by the Spirit, they mortify the sinful nature, they will live. Christianity without mortification is anemic Christianity. That's why the Christian life has sometimes been described as a holy war. As that beautiful hymn "Be Thou My Vision" states,

> Be Thou my Breastplate, my Sword for the fight;
> Be Thou my whole Armor, be Thou my true Might;
> Be Thou my soul's Shelter, be Thou my strong Tow'r,
> O raise Thou me heav'nward, great Pow'r of my pow'r. [8]

Since sin is ugly, the battle is going to be ugly. So we put to death "sexual immorality, impurity, passion, evil desire, and covetousness, which is idolatry" because "the wrath of God is coming" against those who practice such behavior (Col. 3:5–6). Our thoughts, affections, impulses, and so on all must be brought into subjection to Christ and his law. If we are to have the mind of Christ (Phil. 2:5), we cannot have thoughts that lead us away from him or bring dishonor on him. Rather, as those who have been raised with Christ, we seek things above (Col. 3:1). We "take every thought captive" for Christ's sake (2 Cor. 10:5) as we engage in mortification.

Quite frankly, the church has to admit, beginning with her pastors, that the duty to put sin to death has not always been impressed on us adequately or forcefully enough. We need to remember that while it is indeed a painful work, mortification is nevertheless a glorious work that brings honor to the Spirit (for his work in us) and the Son (for giving us the Spirit). As sins are mortified, Christ is glorified. The death of sin in our lives is the vindication of the cross and Christ.

Good Works

Good works are an immensely important aspect of the Christian life. We are God's "workmanship, created in Christ Jesus for good works, which God prepared beforehand, that we should walk in them" (Eph. 2:10). To the degree that we speak negatively about good works, we are speaking negatively about the work of God and the glory of Christ. As we prioritize good works in Christian living, we are giving thanks to God, who gave us these good works, which, as we perform them, lead us back to him in our thoughts and actions.

Christians must, of course, acknowledge that we perform good works because the triune God powerfully indwells us. We are active beings with the divinely given capacity to do real good in this world toward God and our neighbors. Moreover, we can be infallibly persuaded that God will not reject the good works we do for his glory because he cannot reject himself or his works in us. He will not reject the good works he has prepared for us to do.

Paul says that "whatever does not proceed from faith is sin" (Rom. 14:23). Our good works must proceed from faith. When they are done this way, we can be sure they are done from the heart. Christianity is a heart religion, which means the principle by which we aim to please God is through faith, not just at the beginning of our Christian lives but throughout the entire time we live on this present earth. We can thank God for his commandments, including the positive application of his "negative" commandments. So "Do not steal" is also "Give to others."

Thus, we are not left wandering in the dark with no knowledge of what constitutes a good work (Eph. 4:25–32).

Because God has given us a "new heart" (i.e., a heart of flesh), our identity has been radically altered. We are able to please God (1 Thess. 2:4) because we are "in Christ." Paul refers to Christians as "the aroma of Christ to God among those who are being saved" (2 Cor. 2:15). It is an incredible truth that, despite indwelling sin, we are nevertheless referred to, either explicitly or implicitly, as those who are righteous, holy, pure, and good. If we were not identified in those ways, then how could we possibly perform righteous, good, holy, or pure works toward God?

As Christians, we instantly recoil from the idea that we are good. But if we understand our goodness in relation to God's grace, our identity in Christ, and the indwelling of the Spirit, then we can say that we are good to the glory of God. Our Lord explicitly says, "The good person out of his good treasure brings forth good" (Matt. 12:35). We can command only people who are good to do good. Hence, life in Christ is the essential prerequisite for doing good before God.

God also rewards us for the good works he has prepared for us to do. This is a double grace, so to speak. He rewards (or "crowns") his own gifts to us. God rewards those who believe he exists and who seek him out of a true and lively faith (Heb. 11:6). Moses was one such person; he "considered the reproach of Christ greater wealth than the treasures of Egypt, for he was looking to the reward" (Heb. 11:26). As a man of faith, Moses was looking to the reward that came from the hand of God. We should be no different.

God showed his love toward us in sending his only Son. Jesus showed his love toward us in laying down his life for us.

These are truly good works! But God demands a response to such love. Mary, the sister of Martha, showed extravagant love toward Christ. She poured expensive ointment over Christ's head, leading certain onlookers to become indignant. But Jesus called Mary's action a "beautiful thing" (Mark 14:6). She was rewarded by Christ: "And truly, I say to you, wherever the gospel is proclaimed in the whole world, what she has done will be told in memory of her" (Mark 14:9).

Those who put Christ before themselves will be rewarded. As the author of Hebrews states, "God is not unjust so as to overlook your work and the love that you have shown for his name in serving the saints, as you still do" (Heb. 6:10). God is more willing to reward us for our imperfect (but sincere) good works than we are willing to be rewarded. He does not have to reward us, since we cannot merit anything before God. But because of his grace, he delights to give gift upon gift to his children, who are marked by his name.

In Sum

Holiness is a Trinitarian activity. The Father justifies us in the name of Christ, forgiving us for our sins and imputing to us a righteousness that comes through faith in Jesus Christ. Our acceptance before God and our new identity mean that he has separated us for a special service toward his Son by the power of the Spirit. As such, because of indwelling sin, the way we are drawn closer to the Father in the name of Christ is through mortifying our sinful nature by the Spirit. If sin leads us away from God, mortification will necessarily—if it is on God's terms—lead us to God. There is nothing neutral about the Christian life. We progress toward God, on the path of good works, because of who we are and what God has given us from the hand of Christ.

While our holiness is imperfect—though sincere—in this life, we are promised that one day Christ will "present the church to himself in splendor, without spot or wrinkle or any such thing, that she might be holy and without blemish" (Eph. 5:27). The goal of our redemption is that the church may, as the bride of Christ, be presented (publicly) to himself in all her glory and splendor. That glory and splendor is our holiness. God will have an added delight in us at that great day when we will most closely resemble his Son because the Spirit, in accordance with God and Christ's purposes, has so fully renovated us and shaped us into Christ's image that we will have a holiness that answers perfectly to our happiness.

12

Illumination

When God speaks to us, we have a duty to listen. We even have a duty to respond. Besides responding corporately with words of praise and thanksgiving, we must also respond privately in prayer. Christianity in its most basic form, as we have noted, is relational Christianity. God condescends to relate to us by speaking to us in a manner suitable to our condition. Since God is God and we are but dust and ashes, he has made a way for us to know, understand, and love him: he has given us the holy Scriptures and the Holy Spirit. Together, the Scriptures speak infallibly, and the Spirit enables us to receive God's words with faith that leads to understanding. As Anselm, echoing Augustine, famously noted: "I believe in order to understand. For this also I believe,—that unless I believed, I should not understand."[1]

Having received words from God, we are enabled by the Spirit, in a sense, to return with "words from God" in prayer. In essence, the Spirit is the bond of communion between us and the Father and Son. He illuminates our spiritual lives so that without him, we might as well be atheists. All our spiritual life comes from the Spirit.

The Authority of God's Word[2]

As the one who sends his Spirit into our hearts, Christ makes sure that the Spirit performs certain works toward us and in us. One of these works includes what theologians have called *illumination*. Illumination may mean a sort of spiritual enlightening. But it is more than that. To be "illuminated" by the Spirit is something that takes place not simply in the abstract but rather in connection with the truth of God. As John Calvin says,

> The Holy Spirit so inheres in His truth, which He expresses in Scripture, that only when its proper reverence and dignity are given to the Word does the Holy Spirit show forth His power. And what has lately been said—that the Word itself is not quite certain for us unless it be confirmed by the testimony of the Spirit—is not out of accord with these things.[3]

Illumination involves a type of certainty that God's word really is just that: God's word. We are not speaking about the giving of a new revelation. Rather, illumination by the Spirit means not only that we know and love God's words but also that our minds and hearts are given spiritual understanding (1 Cor. 2:14; 2 Cor. 3:14–16; 4:6; Eph. 1:17–18; 3:18–19). Illumination by the Spirit means God's truth is applied to us as revealed truth. Calvin adds,

> For by a kind of mutual bond the Lord has joined together the certainty of his Word and of his Spirit so that the perfect religion of the Word may abide in our minds when the Spirit, who causes us to contemplate God's face, shines; and that we in turn may embrace the Spirit with no fear of being

deceived when we recognize him in his own image, namely, in the Word.[4]

We need to remember that God's instances of revealing himself beyond what is natural (i.e., in creation) concerns supernatural revelation throughout the history of redemption, not all of which has been permanently recorded for us. So, for example, John tells us that Jesus did (and by implication said) many things as supernatural revelation that were never recorded (John 21:25). Indeed, all supernatural revelation requires supernatural illumination for proper understanding. As John Owen notes, Scripture is now the "only external means of divine supernatural illumination, because it is the only repository of all divine supernatural revelation."[5] The Holy Spirit bears witness to the truth of God's word because the Spirit is truth. The internal testimony of the Holy Spirit infallibly assures believers that Scripture is God's word.

The authority of the word of God comes from itself as God's word. Scripture is self-evidencing and possesses an innate efficacy because of its author. Light and power constitute the self-evidencing nature of Scripture as the word of God. Light, like God and Scripture, does not require proof of authenticity. And so Owen refers to the Scriptures as "light," indeed, "a glorious, shining light . . . an illuminating light, compared to and preferred above the light of the sun."[6]

Consequently, the church must hold out the "light" ministerially and declaratively, not legislatively: in other words, the church holds out the light, though the church itself is not the light. Those in the church who have not been blinded by Satan, who have been given a supernatural faith by the Holy Spirit dwelling in them, will readily assent to the Scripture as the word of God because as light, it authenticates itself. Owen continues:

"By this self-evidencing light, I say, doth the Scripture make such a proposition of itself as the word of God, that whoever rejects it, doth it at the peril of his eternal ruin."[7] The other aspect that shows Scripture to be the very word of God is its innate power.

The Scriptures are not read or preached as a naked word but as a word clad with power; the word of God effects change because it is powerful (Acts 20:32; Col. 1:6; James 1:21). Scripture cuts into the hearts of men; it judges and sentences them; it convicts, converts, makes wise, and consoles; in short, its power to effect change in men proves that it is revelation from God.[8] What a source of confidence we have: God still speaks powerfully today because he makes his speech consistent with his nature.

Opening Our Eyes

Spiritual blindness is one of the gravest judgments in God's word (Isa. 6:10; Matt. 15:14; 23:16, 24). If spiritual blindness is a judgment from God, then receiving eyes to see spiritual things is a blessing from God that we should seek. As the psalmist says,

> Open my eyes, that I may behold
>   wondrous things out of your law. (Ps. 119:18)

Nothing grieves a pastor more than seeing willful blindness, but nothing gives a pastor more joy than to watch the spiritually blind come to see Christ.

We depend on God to open our eyes so that we can "behold" the truths contained in his word. When Paul recounts his conversion, he notes his authority, given to him from above, to open the eyes of sinners, "so that they may turn from darkness to light and from the power of Satan to God" (Acts 26:18). Illumination takes place in connection with truth; you cannot have one without the other (Luke 24:45).

The opening of our eyes may also be understood in terms of the darkness-light contrast found in God's word. God calls us "out of darkness into his marvelous light" (1 Pet. 2:9). "Light" has much significance in the Scripture. Besides moral purity, it also has in view "understanding." Jesus came to give us understanding in order to "know him who is true" (1 John 5:20).

Our spiritual blessings in the heavenly places include the Father's gift of "wisdom and of revelation in the knowledge of him" (Eph. 1:17). The Father gives the Holy Spirit in order to enlighten our hearts to know and believe God's truth (Eph. 1:17–18). As Paul says elsewhere, "Now we have received not the spirit of the world, but the Spirit who is from God, that we might understand the things freely given us by God" (1 Cor. 2:12). The understanding lies in our hearts and minds being opened to receive spiritual truth in a manner that leads us to salvation. The Spirit does not come in the name of Christ and perform the work of Christ in our souls in vain. Thomas Goodwin understands Ephesians 1:17 to mean that "every new degree of light adds a further degree of knowledge. Therefore it is said to be by revelation. He would have them to have new sights of God, which might lead them into communion with God."[9]

Without the Spirit, we could not respond in faith and obedience to God's word. The promises of God would be like sawdust in our mouths instead of something sweet. As we receive the word of God in connection with the work of the Spirit, a necessary teaching takes place. God teaches so that we may learn. But God also supplies his Spirit so that our learning is not in vain. Since we have "been anointed by the Holy One," we possess "knowledge" (1 John 2:20). Why do some believe the truths concerning Christ? It can only come down to the reality that Christ sends his Spirit into the hearts of some and not others, for it is not a matter of social class or intelligence that explains why some believe and others do not.

The Holy Spirit and Preaching

Reformation-era theologians generally were united on saying that the faithful preaching of the word of God is the word of God. The Second Helvetic Confession (1566) codified this principle in chapter 1:

> THE PREACHING OF THE WORD OF GOD IS THE WORD OF GOD. Wherefore when this Word of God is now preached in the church by preachers lawfully called, we believe that the very Word of God is proclaimed, and received by the faithful; and that neither any other Word of God is to be invented nor is to be expected from heaven: and that now the Word itself which is preached is to be regarded, not the minister that preaches; for even if he be evil and a sinner, nevertheless the Word of God remains still true and good.[10]

The Second Helvetic Confession is also careful to argue that affirming inward illumination does not negate the need for the preaching of the gospel. The Spirit and the word are friends; they are not ordinarily going to work apart from each other. Thus, when the word is faithfully preached, Christ is speaking through his servant. The Spirit accompanies the truth concerning Christ because that is his work: to testify of the Son. So to reject the word faithfully preached is to reject Christ and thus also to reject the Spirit of Christ (Luke 10:16).

In Romans 10:14–17 Paul makes a number of logical connections, including the reality that for people to believe, they need to hear the word of God preached by those sent by God. We can translate Paul's words in Romans 10:14 as follows: "And how are they to believe him of whom they have never heard?" (my trans.). This means that the preacher is, in a sense, the voice of Christ.

For the minister to be the voice of Christ, he must possess a threefold authority: (1) be lawfully ordained and sent by the church, (2) preach the word of God faithfully, and (3) preach in the demonstration of the Spirit. The apostle Paul notes that he was called by God in his office as apostle (1 Cor. 1:1) before later adding that he proclaimed nothing but "Jesus Christ and him crucified" in the "demonstration of the Spirit and of power" so that his hearers, who received his words by faith, would rest in God's power (1 Cor. 2:1–5; see also 1 Thess. 1:5–6).

It does not matter if an angel from heaven should preach the words of God: if the Spirit does not accompany such preaching, it will fail to have any positive effect on the hearers. Instead, people will be as moved as the chairs they sit on. But on the other hand, when the truth is accurately preached (even by a wicked man), and the Spirit works the truth in our hearts, minds, and souls, we can confidently say with Paul, "And we also thank God constantly for this, that when you received the word of God, which you heard from us, you accepted it not as the word of men but as what it really is, the word of God, which is at work in you believers" (1 Thess. 2:13).

The Spirit brings about a holy submission in God's people so that when God's word is preached and Christ is exalted in that proclamation, the faithful will always respond—even if they are convicted of their sin—in a manner whereby we can say the word is powerfully at work.

The Holy Spirit and Prayer[11]

One of the greatest blessings we can receive from God is the Spirit (not "a spirit") of supplication. When God pours out his

Spirit in the Old Testament, it usually indicates a reference to his Spirit (Ezek. 39:29; Joel 2:28–29). The Spirit gives grace and enables us to cry for mercy (Zech. 12:10). The Spirit not only enables us to pray but works in us the right types of affections needed for communion with God in prayer.

In our discussion on the Trinity-oriented life, we considered prayers directed *to* the Spirit as the third person of the Trinity. Our focus here is on praying *in* the Spirit as the one who fills us and empowers our prayers. Sometimes God's people are peculiarly blessed by an outpouring of the Spirit so that their wills and affections are more sensitive to the things of God and they have an unnatural boldness in making requests to God. In fact, when we pray in the Spirit, which is the only way to pray, we find that he helps us in our weakness:

> For we do not know what to pray for as we ought, but the Spirit himself intercedes for us with groanings too deep for words. And he who searches hearts knows what is the mind of the Spirit, because the Spirit intercedes for the saints according to the will of God. (Rom 8:26–27)

He works as our advocate on earth and enables us to pray in a manner that satisfies God because we are praying according to his will. We cannot always understand or know where our prayers will take us, but being firmly rooted in his word and depending on the Spirit of supplication, we have confidence that we will be heard, because we are speaking not strictly on our own but as those who have an intercessor on earth whose will is the same as our intercessor's will in heaven.

We are assured that our Father hears us because our cries to God the Father are from the Spirit: "For you did not receive the spirit of slavery to fall back into fear, but you have received the

Spirit of adoption as sons, by whom we cry, 'Abba! Father!'"
(Rom. 8:15; see also Gal. 4:6).

Prayer is not easy. Listen to John Bunyan:

> May I but speak my own Experience, and from that tell
> you the difficulty of Praying to God as I ought; it is enough
> to make you poor, blind, carnal men, to entertain strange
> thoughts of me. For, as for my heart, when I go to pray, I
> find it so reluctant to go to God, and when it is with him, so
> reluctant to stay with him, that many times I am forced in my
> Prayers; *first* to beg God that he would take mine heart, and
> set it on himself in Christ, and when it is there, that he would
> keep it there. In fact, many times I know not what to pray for,
> I am so blind, nor how to pray, I am so ignorant; only (blessed
> be Grace) the *Spirit helps our infirmities* [Rom. 8:26].[12]

If the Spirit did not "excite" us to prayer and help us in our
infirmities, we would have zero communion with God. Even
with the Spirit, in these bodies where so much indwelling sin
remains, we are poor, pitiful creatures at times.

As a pastor, I'm concerned how many Christians have such
energy for the things of the world. We will drive across town
for our kids to get to piano lessons or take them to soccer practice, but we seem very often to have little energy for the things
of God. Each day we must deny ourselves, take up our crosses,
and follow Christ (Luke 9:23). Each day we must seek first the
kingdom of God (Matt. 6:33). But why is it that once a month
or once a week we find it so difficult to meet together to pray
corporately? For all the "gospel-centered" talk about this and
that, why has corporate prayer fallen on hard times? What are
we doing that is more important than praying together?

The Scriptures seem to me to be very clear on the nature and
necessity of corporate prayer meetings:

> All these with one accord were devoting themselves to prayer, together with the women and Mary the mother of Jesus, and his brothers. (Acts 1:14)

> When he realized this, he went to the house of Mary, the mother of John whose other name was Mark, where many were gathered together and were praying. (Acts 12:12)

Corporate prayer suffers in the North American church especially because people have not known the holiness and goodness of God in personal prayer. Perhaps they haven't asked enough of God and thus haven't received the answers he is so willing to give (Matt. 7:7–8; 18:19; 21:22; Mark 11:24)? They haven't personally grasped the value of prayer and how important it is for our souls. Thus they are decidedly unmoved in wanting to meet for corporate prayer because the problem begins in private. Perhaps there is a correlation between private and public laziness in the church today? But corporate prayer will help our private prayer, and vice versa. We need both because the Christian life involves both (Matt. 6:4–6; Acts 12:12). And I think pastors who don't meet to pray with their people need to have a compelling reason why they don't.

Those who have met with God their Father in private prayer should also desire to meet with God "our Father" among the brothers and sisters. After all, the church is a body (i.e., a family), which thrives in unity and in numbers (Matt. 18:20; Acts 1:14).

The well-known New England Puritan Thomas Shepard remarked that even among the best Christians there are times when they would rather die than pray.[13] Often I don't feel like praying privately, and sometimes I don't feel like praying corporately. But it is a Christian duty. And often, in his grace, God turns my duties into delights (or partial delights). But there's something much more important than the blessing I receive: there's the advancement of Christ's kingdom and glory when his saints gather together and call on the name of the Lord (i.e., pray the first three petitions of the Lord's Prayer). And for that reason we ought always to be praying together (Acts 2:42).

Satan hates private prayer. But I suspect he hates corporate prayer even more. And when the Spirit is present in our corporate prayer, Satan is least "happy." It seems he might be winning many battles in the church today that he has no business winning. One of those is keeping the godly from praying with each other in the Spirit. Life is just a little too easy for us in North America, so the need to pray is not as pressing as it might be for Christians in countries that feel greater hardships or in eras when times were more difficult.

How sad that God desires to bless us but that we act as if we do not need to be blessed. God and Christ are willing to open the floodgates of heaven to a praying people, but we must ask, or we will not receive. But even more important, should we not, as the body of Christ, be asking for the head to receive his glory, power, and dominion?

Henry Scudder, a Westminster divine, made the provocative but theologically accurate point that "prayer, because it is ordained by God, and has his promise, calls in, and engages in God's power and truth for him that makes it, and so through God becomes omnipotent."[14] Imagine that: prayer, through God, becomes omnipotent!

Christ's Vicar

Let us rejoice, as we have Christ's vicar (representative) on earth not in the form of a man (i.e., the pope) but in the person of the Spirit, the third person of the Trinity. As John Owen observes, the Holy Spirit "supplies the *bodily absence* of Christ" and by him fulfills "all his promises to the church."[15] Similarly, Richard Sibbes declares, "Christ is always with his church from the beginning of the world, and will be to the end"; all that Christ does for the church is done "as he hath the Spirit."[16]

As our Guide and Comforter, the Spirit illumines our hearts and minds to receive Christ from God. The bodily absence of Christ is real, but that is not a problem for us who possess the Holy Spirit. What Jesus desires from us is belief in his name and all that glorifies him by way of the truth. He is not going to leave that to chance. He sends the Spirit to make sure that we are not left as orphans but that we are here on earth as children of the Father, who cry out in the Spirit through our prayers and supplications.

Christianity emphasizes the work of the Holy Spirit because the true work of the Spirit is the work of Christ on earth post-ascension. To the end that we have rightly understood the Spirit, we have also rightly understood the one who stands at the center of our confession. One of the surest ways to discern whether a church is Spirit filled is to ask, To what degree is that same church also Christ exalting in the content of its worship and preaching? There is necessarily a connection between the two because God has made that connection. And what God has joined together, let not man separate!

PART 4

THE CHURCH-INHABITED LIFE

13

Structure

Historically, Protestants have placed a great value on the importance of the local, visible church. Indeed, the Puritan movement arose mainly because of the desire by godly men to reform the Church of England in ways consistent with the word of God. Ministers were prepared to give up everything for this cause because, as they saw it, without a healthy church, there could be no healthy Christians.

In what is surely one of the most famous statements on the glories of the church, Cyprian (ca. 200–258) writes,

> The spouse of Christ cannot be adulterous; she is uncorrupted and pure. She knows one home; she guards with chaste modesty the sanctity of one couch. She keeps us for God. She appoints the sons whom she has born for the kingdom. Whoever is separated from the Church and is joined to an adulteress, is separated from the promises of the Church; nor can he who forsakes the Church of Christ attain to the rewards of Christ. He is a stranger; he is profane; he is an enemy. He can no longer have God for his Father, who has not the Church for his mother.[1]

There is obviously a context to Cyprian's belief, but generally speaking, if you wish to have God as your Father, you must have the church as your mother. John Calvin affirmed this principle again during the Reformation:

> I shall start, then, with the church, into whose bosom God is pleased to gather his sons, not only that they may be nourished by her help and ministry as long as they are infants and children, but also that they may be guided by her motherly care until they mature and at last reach the goal of faith . . . so that, for those to whom he is Father the church may also be Mother. And this was so not only under the law but also after Christ's coming, as Paul testifies when he teaches that we are the children of the new and heavenly Jerusalem (Gal. 4:26).[2]

Basically, we can all agree that a good mother protects, nourishes, and strengthens her children. When those children are God's children, the responsibility of the "mother" (i.e., the church) is naturally enhanced to such a degree that we talk about the necessity of the church in terms of life and death. As a baby starves to death without milk from its mother, a person will spiritually starve without the milk of God's word from the church. In other words, you cannot be a private Christian. The New Testament especially makes Christianity a "public" matter in which believers belong to a visible assembly of God's people, which ordinarily includes pastors, elders, deacons, and members.

The People of God

The church is the people of God, the body of Christ, who worship (and live) by the Spirit according to truth. From the beginning, Adam belonged to God. He was God's son. If he had not fallen, his children would have likewise been sons of God by natural propagation. The fall in Genesis 3 did not, however, obliterate God's purpose to have children on earth. With the promise of the Messiah in Genesis 3:15, all who would belong to God would be identified as those whose hope and trust was in a second Adam who could bring them to God.

God has a people who belong to him: "And I will walk among you and will be your God, and you shall be my people" (Lev. 26:12). God refers to his people as his "treasured possession": "For you are a people holy to the LORD your God. The LORD your God has chosen you to be a people for his treasured possession, out of all the peoples who are on the face of the earth" (Deut. 7:6; see also Deut. 14:2; 26:18; Ps. 135:4; Mal. 3:17; Titus 2:14).

Just as Adam was God's son, now Israel takes on that identity (Ex. 4:22; Hos. 11:1). Ultimately, in the New Testament, especially in the Gospels, we see Jesus reconstituting Israel around himself. Jesus is Israel called out of Egypt (Matt. 2:15), for he is the true Son of God. All the Old Testament institutions concerning worship are fulfilled in Christ, who is the new tabernacle (John 1:14; Acts 15:16–17), the new temple (John 2:19–21; Eph. 2:19–22), the founder of the twelve new tribes (Matt. 10:1–4; Rev. 21:12–14), and one who represents Israel's eschatological resurrection hope (Acts 26:6–8). Only he can displace Jerusalem as the place of worship (John 4:20–24) by forming an enhanced (new) body of true worshipers (Phil. 3:3). He brings these worshipers to the true, new Jerusalem on Mount Zion (Gal. 4:25–26; Heb. 12:22). The old shadowy Jerusalem has been replaced with the real, heavenly Jerusalem (Rev. 21), which will one day come down to earth.

All who belong to Christ are the elect, the chosen (Col. 3:12). Those who worship by the Spirit, in the name of Christ, are the true circumcision (Phil. 3:3), because they worship God in heaven by the Spirit and have been cleansed. Edmund Clowney speaks of our worship on earth in relation to heaven with these excellent observations:

> We assemble here on earth (Heb. 10:25) because we assemble there, where Jesus is. Christians share in the inheritance of the saints in light (Col. 1:12); their life is already in heaven with Christ (Col. 3:1–4). Christ is the head of his body as a heavenly assembly (Col. 1:18 . . .). When the Corinthian Christians come together in assembly (1 Cor. 11:18; 14:26, 28), they join with "all those everywhere who call on the name of our Lord Jesus Christ" (1 Cor. 1:2). Not only do we come to the assembly where our risen Lord is; he comes by his Spirit to the assembly where we are.[3]

All this is to argue that the people of God are one body. Peter does his best to convince his readers of the unity of God's people when he writes,

> But you are a chosen race, a royal priesthood, a holy nation, a people for his own possession, that you may proclaim the excellencies of him who called you out of darkness into his marvelous light. Once you were not a people, but now you are God's people; once you had not received mercy, but now you have received mercy. (1 Pet. 2:9–10)

Peter takes Old Testament language (e.g., Ex. 19:5–6) that described the people of God and applies it to the people of God in the new covenant, which includes Gentiles. Gentiles have not replaced Jews, but rather, they have been engrafted into the people of God, which includes believing Jews and now believing Gentiles—all of whom are saved by the same precious blood of Christ.

Church Membership[4]

For all these delightful descriptions of the redeemed as the bride and body of Christ, the people of God, God's treasured possession, and so on, there is the matter of how one belongs to the visible church on earth. We inhabit the church on earth (and will one day inhabit the church in the heavenly places), but our admittance to the church is never purely a personal decision. Spiritual "keys" have been granted to the church so that God's people may be publicly brought into the church.

Yet the question must be asked, To whom do the keys of the kingdom belong (Matt. 16:17–19)? All the members of the whole body are the recipients of the power described, for the "power of the whole is in every part," Thomas Peck writes.[5] This means that the body possesses power insofar as the members elect church officers (Acts 6:3; 14:23; Titus 1:5), whereas the officers possess power as to its exercise. Only the elders, as elected by and representative of the members of the church, have the power to "bind" and "loose" (Matt. 16:19). Elders have ministerial and declarative power, not legislative power. They simply execute the law of Christ. In each church a plurality of elders is assumed or commanded (Acts 20:28; Phil. 1:1; 1 Thess. 5:12–13; Titus 1:5; 1 Pet. 5:1–2). These elders may be either teaching elders or ruling elders (1 Tim. 5:17).

Some not only disagree with God-appointed shepherds having this type of God-given authority but also deny that church membership is required or biblical. First, we should admit that we are members of the body and that this is true of each person who belongs to Christ: "We are members of his body" (Eph. 5:30). What is true "invisibly" must have a corresponding "visible" reality.

Without church membership, doubt ensues; without church membership, accountability between both pastors and sheep is jettisoned. In Hebrews 13:17 the author writes,

> Obey your leaders and submit to them, for they are keeping watch over your souls, as those who will have to give an account. Let them do this with joy and not with groaning, for that would be of no advantage to you.

Readers are aware that they have specific leaders to whom they must obey and submit. These leaders keep watch over their souls. Without church membership, whereby the leaders and the sheep are aware of this relationship, how can one possibly submit to one's leaders? How can leaders be aware of which people they must account for before Almighty God? And how can Christians know which ordained leaders they need to submit to?

The Christian faith must take seriously the requirements for belonging to the local church. What are they?

Speaking from a Presbyterian viewpoint, Guy Waters observes,

> Presbyterianism is essential to the well-being (*bene esse*) but not to the essence (*esse*) of the church. Nonacceptance of Presbyterianism is, therefore, no barrier to receiving a non-Presbyterian person as a Christian, or a non-Presbyterian church as a true branch of the church, provided that he in fact holds fast the only Head of the church, Jesus Christ.[6]

Thus, in my own denomination, the Presbyterian Church in America, for example, we welcome as a communicant member anyone who makes a simple, credible profession of faith in Jesus

Christ—someone embracing the tenets of the Christian faith in basic form. If someone belongs to Christ, we have no grounds for barring him or her from visible communion in Christ's body. Our desire for unity—objectified in our terms for membership— is our glory and Christ's glory (John 17:20–22).

The terms for membership are expressed in the following questions from the Presbyterian Church in America's *Book of Church Order* (sec. 57-5):

1. Do you acknowledge yourself to be a sinner in the sight of God, justly deserving His displeasure, and without hope save in His sovereign mercy?
2. Do you believe in the Lord Jesus Christ as the Son of God, and Savior of sinners, and do you receive and rest upon Him alone for salvation as He is offered in the Gospel?
3. Do you now resolve and promise, in humble reliance upon the grace of the Holy Spirit, that you will endeavor to live as becomes the followers of Christ?
4. Do you promise to support the Church in its worship and work to the best of your ability?
5. Do you submit yourself to the government and discipline of the Church, and promise to study its purity and peace?

This form of ecclesiology has some advantages. For example, this position on the requirements for members refrains from sectarianism. There is a healthy catholicity to this ecclesiology, which is seen in the denomination's Communion practice. Christianity insists on the fact that we are sinners who believe in Jesus Christ alone for our salvation and also that we cannot obey and please God apart from the grace of the Holy Spirit. But Christianity is also church inhabited, insofar as those who make these great professions are committed to the local church and submit to her leaders who have been appointed by Christ.

If one belongs to Christ, then one must belong to the local church. One's Communion practice ought to be consistent with this principle, insisting that the "gates" to the Lord's Table are as wide as the "gates" to heaven. In other words, if someone is going to heaven, then who are we to forbid him from coming to partake of the one who is Lord of heaven and earth? We have no authority to bar from the table someone whom Christ has welcomed. Whatever errors she may or may not have in her theology, her profession of faith in the Savior, by the Spirit, is the sine qua non of salvation (Rom. 10:8–9).

The church is a place for sinners who have been redeemed by the precious blood of Christ. Leaders ought to trust that the church is the place to nurture and teach the redeemed. The church (formally) accepts all who belong to Christ, but that does not mean that the teachers and leaders in the church do not make it their aim to instruct God's (sometimes spiritually immature) people while they are already members of the church (Heb. 5:12–6:3).

The Church as Mother

As noted earlier in chapter 2, public worship is the zenith of our Christian experience insofar as we never better represent who we are than when we are worshiping, as the body, the one who is our head. The church is our mother, taking care of our spiritual needs in ways that only the body can.

Acts 2:42 records that the early Christians "devoted themselves to the apostles' teaching and the fellowship, to the breaking of bread and the prayers." The believers were "together" and attended the temple together; they broke bread together in their homes (Acts 2:44–46). These people were not only accountable to each other but were to exhort one another (Heb. 3:13). In Romans 12 we have a sort of blueprint for congregational life based on the various giftings we have received from the Lord:

> For as in one body we have many members, and the members do not all have the same function, so we, though many, are one body in Christ, and individually members one of another. Having gifts that differ according to the grace given to us, let us use them: if prophecy, in proportion to our faith; if service, in our serving; the one who teaches, in his teaching; the one who exhorts, in his exhortation; the one who contributes, in generosity; the one who leads, with zeal; the one who does acts of mercy, with cheerfulness. (Rom. 12:4–8)

Life in the church is the spiritual medicine we need in order to stay healthy. One of the strongest warnings found anywhere in the Bible is issued to professing Christians in Hebrews 10:25, where they are exhorted not to neglect meeting together. Immediately before that, however, we are given one reason why we should not give up meeting together: "And let us consider how to stir up one another to love and good works" (10:24). How can we possibly stir up (Gk. *eis paroxysmos*, "to incite or stimulate") another person to love and good works if we are not present to do so? Exhortation, encouragement, and empathy are some of the virtues that should be present in a relationship between members of the body.

In the Apostles' Creed, we confess that we believe in the "communion of saints," which the Westminster Confession of Faith takes up and identifies as "all saints . . . united to Jesus Christ their Head, by his Spirit, and by faith" (26.1), and, more summarily, as "all those who, in every place, call upon the name of the Lord Jesus" (26.2). Notice that the creed and confession see this "communion" as referring to believers in Christ from every place and era. The substance of this communion is that all Christians "have fellowship with him in his graces, sufferings, death, resurrection, and glory: and, being united to one another in love, they have communion in each other's gifts and graces." The responsibility of this communion concerns the fact that Christians are "obliged to the performance of such duties, public and private, as do conduce to their mutual good, both in the inward and outward man" (26.1).

We believe in the communion of saints because we believe that we are to love one another and do good to all people, especially those who belong to Christ (Gal. 6:10). The faithful preaching of God's word, as well as the worthy receiving of the sacraments, enables us to show true love to God and our neighbor. When Christ's person and work are proclaimed from the pulpit, we are better equipped to obey Paul's commands in Philippians 2:3–4, where he writes, "Do nothing from selfish ambition or conceit, but in humility count others more significant than yourselves. Let each of you look not only to his own interests, but also to the interests of others."

Again, these commands require two things: (1) a community of people so that we can perform the obedience required and (2) a Savior who gives us the proper reason or basis for why we should. Christ's life and death provide for us the perfect example of humility and service for others. If we belong to Christ, we will likewise show humility and love toward our neighbors, because our eyes are on the Lord.

Conclusion

Our identity as the fullness of Christ (Eph. 1:21), the body of our Lord, the chosen of God explains why we are able to worship and offer ourselves as acceptable sacrifices to God (Rom. 12:1). We do this in the context of the church so that we can say that our Christian lives are church inhabited. We flee for refuge on the Lord's Day to the household of God so that we may ascend the hill of the Lord (Pss. 15:1; 24:3) and worship with those with whom we share the same identity, namely, children of the living God.

Our union with Christ, and thus with each other, means that we have obligations not only to glorify Christ but also to serve one another in ways that will lead to mutual spiritual edification. God has gifted to us the church of Jesus Christ, so that, ordinarily speaking, there is no salvation outside the visible, local church.[7]

You cannot love Christ and hate his bride. You cannot have God as your Father without having the church as your mother. Perhaps nothing would reveal pride as much as people who determine in their heart that they do not need the church. Thankfully, God has given us the Spirit so that we may know and believe that nothing that God has given us is to be rejected, but rather, all is to be received with thanksgiving and used to its appropriate end.

14

Worship

Christianity makes a big deal of corporate worship. When the church gathers on the Lord's Day, we do so primarily to worship God. We come to the Father in the name of Christ by the power of the Spirit, and we do so in a manner acceptable to God, with reverence and awe. Worship, as glorious as it is, is not easy. And by worship, we are not speaking strictly about the praise and worship songs in a church service but about everything from the call to worship to the closing benediction.

Christian worship can be very appealing, even to the ungodly. For example, Ezekiel's preaching was deeply satisfying in a carnal manner to his hearers (Ezek. 33:31–32). Herod heard John the Baptist gladly (Mark 6:20). Saint John Chrysostom's preaching caused his hearers to clap for him; on one occasion he preached a sermon against clapping, and his audience continued to clap at his inspiring oratory.

We need to ask ourselves whether we are coming for the ordinances (e.g., preaching, sacraments, hymns) or for communion with God through the ordinances. We can do our daily Bible reading each day—according to Robert Murray M'Cheyne's calendar, for instance—and miss communing with God in the reading of our Bibles. This happens corporately as well as individually. God describes the people during Isaiah's time in a rather heartbreaking way, noting that many of his people

> draw near with their mouth
>> and honor me with their lips,
>> while their hearts are far from me. (Isa. 29:13)

The point of worship is to bring us to God, for that is why Christ died: "For Christ also suffered once for sins, the righteous for the unrighteous, that he might bring us to God" (1 Pet. 3:18). We come, by faith, to draw near to God, not simply to "go to church." As the author of Hebrews states, "And without faith it is impossible to please him, for whoever would draw near to God must believe that he exists and that he rewards those who seek him" (Heb. 11:6).

What we find in the Scriptures are many good and helpful principles concerning how corporate worship ought to be conducted. While there is some genuine liberty in how we order our corporate worship, there are certain nonnegotiable elements that should characterize worship among God's people over the ages and in different places.

Dialogue

Worship is covenantal insofar as God covenants with us through Jesus Christ to bless us and make us in the image of his Son. We become like what we worship (Ps. 115:8), which means for Christians we can have no option other than to worship Jesus. Worship creates "two-way traffic" between the human soul and the triune God. It is shaped in the form of a dialogue: God speaks to us, and we speak to God.

Worship is for the redeemed. After Noah and his family had been saved through the waters of baptism, God called Noah and his family out of the ark (Gen. 8:15–16)—a "call to worship." Noah responded to God's call to come out with worship: "Then Noah built an altar to the LORD and took some of every clean animal and some of every clean bird and offered burnt offerings on the altar" (Gen. 8:20). God then responded to Noah's worship with a promise:

> And when the LORD smelled the pleasing aroma, the LORD said in his heart, "I will never again curse the ground because of man. . . . Neither will I ever again strike down every living creature as I have done." (Gen. 8:21)

Noah and his family were the visible church at this point in redemptive history. God continued to speak to Noah regarding both promises and commands, which are integral aspects of true worship. Careful readers of the Scriptures can find the "dialogical principle" throughout God's word, which is simply this: God speaks, and we respond. God speaks in light of who he is and what he has done, and we respond back to God by praising him not only for who he is and what he has done but also for what we will do as the redeemed.

Public Worship

The worship that the Bible focuses on is both public and corporate. Even in the beginning of redemptive history, the first worship war is public, involving Cain and his brother Abel. In the Psalms there is an accent on corporate worship, such as in Psalm 95:6–7:

> Oh come, let us worship and bow down;
>> let us kneel before the LORD, our Maker!
> For he is our God,
>> and we are the people of his pasture,
>> and the sheep of his hand.

In the New Testament, nothing changes in terms of the corporate and public nature of worship. God's people, now consisting also of Gentiles, meet together to worship God:

> They devoted themselves to the apostles' teaching and the fellowship, to the breaking of bread and the prayers. . . . And day by day, attending the temple together and breaking bread in their homes, they received their food with glad and generous hearts, praising God and having favor with all the people. And the Lord added to their number day by day those who were being saved. (Acts 2:42, 46–47)

Christians did not die in the early church because they worshiped alone in their hearts; they died because of the public nature of their confession as worshipers of the true and living God, who is the Father of our Lord Jesus Christ.

In one of the most terrifying warnings offered anywhere in holy Scripture, the author of Hebrews exhorts his readers to hold fast to their confession and trust in God's faithfulness toward them (Heb. 10:23). He then proceeds to exhort them "to stir up one another to love and good works" (10:24). But then he warns them not to neglect to meet together, "as is the habit of some" (10:25). When the author speaks of "sinning deliberately after receiving the knowledge of the truth" (10:26), he is addressing professing Christians who have stopped worshiping publicly and corporately. Such can only expect "a fearful expectation of judgment, and a fury of fire" (10:27). Corporate worship, ordinarily speaking, is not optional for the Christian.

Christ's Gifts

Why is it such a heinous sin to neglect to worship God with his people? There are a host of reasons. One could argue that it is impossible to obey Romans 14 on dealing with weaker brothers if you are never around weaker brothers. One could also argue that you cannot stir up others to good works or encourage others if you are willfully separating yourself from the people of God. But one could also note that by neglecting worship you are showing contempt for Christ's gifts that he gave to the church.

In Ephesians 4:7–8, where Paul quotes Psalm 68:18, we read,

> But grace was given to each one of us according to the measure of Christ's gift. Therefore it says,
>
> > "When he ascended on high he led a host of captives,
> >   and he gave gifts to men."

Jesus, the ascended Lord of glory, did not leave the church helpless. He gave gifts to the church, since he is the husband taking care of the bride (see Rom. 12:6–8; 1 Cor. 12:8–11, 28; Eph. 4:11; 1 Pet. 4:11). Jesus gave apostles, prophets, evangelists, shepherds, and teachers "to equip the saints for the work of ministry, for building up the body of Christ" (Eph. 4:11–12). Where do these various people, who have been called to these offices, exercise their gifts primarily? They do so in the context of the visible church in order that, among other things, God's people are not "tossed to and fro by the waves and carried about by every wind of doctrine" (Eph. 4:14). The body grows, as the new temple, into maturity through public worship where teaching takes place. These teachers are gifts to the church from Christ himself and are therefore to be respected and obeyed (Heb. 13:17).

Elements

Since Christ gifts teachers to the church, worship necessarily involves a component of teaching. In terms of the dialogical principle, teachers are the mouthpieces of Christ. Preaching and the reading of God's word, which are both crucial aspects of public worship, are God's way of speaking to us (1 Thess. 2:13). Since we worship in the Spirit and in truth (John 4:24), the truth must be proclaimed and read. God must speak! We pray, with thanksgivings and supplications, as our way of responding to God. We also sing songs of praise to God as a way to speak to him his truth that has gripped our hearts and minds.

From the New Testament, we see that certain elements (e.g., preaching and prayer) must be included in worship. Outside of the elements required, nothing else should be allowed. We must allow God to determine how we worship, but rest assured, he does so not only for his glory but also for our benefit. Indeed, there are certain liberties in matters indifferent, in how we structure worship or the types of songs we sing, for example, but there are also certain patterns and commandments that are not optional.[1] So we can see that Paul regulates prayer (1 Cor. 11:2–16; 14:14–17; 1 Tim. 2:8), singing (1 Cor. 14:26–27; Eph. 5:19; Col. 3:16), the ministry of the word (1 Cor. 14:29–33; 1 Tim. 4:13; 2 Tim. 4:1–2), the collection (1 Cor. 16:1–2), and the Lord's Supper (1 Cor. 11:17–34).

We live in God's presence. But in a special way, unique to God's people, we worship in his presence. He must be allowed to speak, for he is the king, and we are his subjects. The more God's word is shoved out the door, only to be replaced by more of our words, the more we are shoving God out the door of our churches.

There is such a thing as false worship, which is usually based on ignorance and unbelief; for example, Jesus said of the Samaritans in his day, "You worship what you do not know" (John 4:22; cf. Gen. 4:3–8; Ex. 32; Lev. 10:1–3). But there is also true worship, as Jesus described: "True worshipers will worship the Father in [the Spirit] and truth, for the Father is seeking such people to worship him" (John 4:23). God does not leave worship to our imaginations but determines that our worship should be done in the Spirit and based on the truth. The Spirit honors the truth because all truth comes from Christ and leads to Christ.

Ordered, Trinitarian Worship

Liturgy is still a nasty word among many Bible-believing evangelicals. Many disputes can be avoided with a little common sense and definition of terms. If we speak of an "order of worship," then we are discoursing on liturgy. And let us face facts: almost all churches have some type of order in their worship. A call to worship (Ps. 95:6) should ordinarily begin a worship service, if we are concerned for some type of order, as Paul was (1 Cor. 14:40). We may wish to emphasize that we are sinners after the reading of God's law, or we may wish to read God's law after an admission of sin and guilt so that we may aim to keep God's law. There is no set liturgy handed down to us that means we cannot have some diversity. We also, as noted above, may wish to follow a dialogical structure, whereby God speaks (call to worship), we respond (prayer), God speaks (reading of the word), we respond (hymn or song of praise), God speaks (preaching), we respond (hymn), God speaks (Lord's Supper), we respond (hymn), and God speaks (benediction).

But in our liturgy (or order of worship), we must still be concerned to maintain a Trinitarian focus wherever possible. Paul says in Ephesians 2:18, "For through [Christ] we both have access in one Spirit to the Father." This is the way we approach God. Jews and Gentiles are united in a common approach to the triune God. Hence, when we baptize in corporate worship, we have a glorious opportunity to highlight the doctrine of the Trinity, not simply because we baptize in the name of the Father, Son, and Holy Spirit but also because we are anticipating, in hopeful dependence on God's grace, that the Father is speaking to his child words of grace, which are effectual because of the outpouring of the Spirit from the hand of the Son (see Matt. 3:16–17). The public Christian life begins in the assembly of God's people with baptism. God's triune name is "stamped" on his people. Baptism symbolizes the adoption by the Father in the name of his Son by the washing of the Spirit (regeneration).

We should also aim to sing hymns that draw our minds to the triunity of God. "Holy, Holy, Holy," for example, does this as well as any hymn:

> Holy, Holy, Holy! Lord God Almighty!
> Early in the morning our song shall rise to Thee.
> Holy, Holy, Holy! Merciful and mighty!
> God in three persons, blessed Trinity![2]

Or "Come, Thou Almighty King":

Come, Thou Almighty King,
help us Thy name to sing,
help us to praise:
Father, all glorious,
o'er all victorious,
come and reign over us,
Ancient of Days.

Come, Thou Incarnate Word,
gird on Thy mighty sword,
our pray'r attend;
Come, and Thy people bless,
and give Thy Word success:
Spirit of holiness,
on us descend.

Come, Holy Comforter,
Thy sacred witness bear
in this glad hour:
Thou who almighty art,
now rule in ev'ry heart,
and ne'er from us depart,
Spirit of pow'r.

To the great One in Three,
eternal praises be
hence evermore.
His sov'reign majesty
may we in glory see,
and to eternity
love and adore.[3]

Hymns of this nature can serve the church in unique ways.[4] For example, God's people can together express the truth of God's word; they can set forth, positively, a theology of what is true. Another way to think of the value of hymn singing is that it distinguishes our theology from the aberrant theologies of various unorthodox groups who may be happy to sing some of the actual words of Scripture, while meaning something quite different by them. The meaning of the words is as important as the words themselves. We are, in our singing, defending the truth of God in a corporate manner.

Moreover, hymn singing is really no different from confessing the Apostles' Creed or Nicene Creed. They are essentially the same thing. We are able to look at truth that has stood the test of time and confess it before God. We are confessing in our singing not the words of man but the truth of God. Thus, singing "Holy, Holy, Holy" or "Come, Thou Almighty King" provides the church with an excellent tool to convey, state, defend, and enjoy the truth of God's word in a manner that even preaching and praying cannot.

Besides our hymns, the nature and content of our prayers ought to highlight the Trinity. In prayer we are making known our desires to God in the name of Christ by the enabling of the Holy Spirit. But our content should also draw people to the tri-unity of God. It should make a great difference to our corporate worship if the confession of God's triunity disappeared. We may need to ask ourselves, What difference would it make to our public worship if we did not speak of the Trinity? Imagine removing the Trinitarian emphasis from Ephesians 1! Likewise, as we saw earlier, it is entirely appropriate to pray to our triune God in general and to each of the three persons specifically, even as we do in song with the hymn "Come, Thou Almighty King" above.

A Trinitarian conception of worship, therefore, recognizes two movements:

1. God toward humanity: from the Father through the Son by the Spirit
2. Humanity toward God (in reverse): by the Spirit through the Son to the Father

This is mere Christianity: worship of the triune God. If our doctrine of Christ and the Holy Spirit cannot lead us to the place where, in corporate worship, we are explicitly and fervently praising the triune God, then we may need to check what type of Christology and pneumatology we have been indoctrinated with. As I see it, worship is where the best theology takes place. And if that isn't focused on the Father, Son, and Holy Spirit, then our worship needs serious reevaluation in light of God's word.

15

Washed

We usually wash (i.e., clean ourselves) before we eat (i.e., nourish ourselves). That statement should help us understand the two sacraments given to us by Christ. The Bible speaks of multiple types of "washings," but the preeminent visible symbol of washing from above is the sacrament of baptism in the name of the triune God.

Baptism symbolizes the whole of salvation. A thorough discussion on baptism should be a thorough discussion on the gospel. Water baptism is representative of Christ's work for sinners. Baptism thus represents not only the washing away of our sins but also our new obedience. As a principal part of our obedience, we believe God's promises to us in Christ by the power of the Spirit. Our life is Trinitarian because our baptism, which we are to continually look to, is Trinitarian.

The Christian faith places such significance on baptism because of all that it represents. We may speak of the duty to be baptized but only after we have spoken of the privilege to be baptized. Few things in the Christian life are as helpful to our walk, assurance, and perseverance as a lively faith that embraces all that baptism promises us through Christ Jesus. To the extent that we neglect a robust understanding of the meaning of baptism, we will impoverish our faith.

We know that the great Reformer Martin Luther frequently appealed to his baptism in his battles against sin and the devil. Luther said, "The only way to drive away the Devil is through faith in Christ, by saying: 'I have been baptized, I am a Christian.'"[1] When by faith we look to our baptism, we believe in the person and work of Christ; we are putting forth acts of faith directed toward our Savior. But what is baptism and its meaning?

Pre-Christian Baptism

Christian baptism is not a rite without a historical predecessor. Unless one has a pretty firm grasp of the Old Testament context and its various ceremonies associated with baptism, he or she is going to have an incomplete picture of its meaning and significance in the New Testament.

The last old covenant prophet, John the Baptist, baptized repentant Israelites in the Jordan (Mark 1). John was in the wilderness, and faithful Israelites went out to him to receive a baptism of repentance and forgiveness of sins (Mark 1:4). This baptism anticipated a different type of baptism, one that would come from Jesus, who would baptize people with the Holy Spirit (Mark 1:8).

In the Old Testament there were various baptisms and cleansings (Heb. 9:10). We see this carried over into the New Testament:

> For the Pharisees and all the Jews do not eat unless they wash their hands properly, holding to the tradition of the elders, and when they come from the marketplace, they do

not eat unless they wash. And there are many other tradi-
tions that they observe, such as the washing of cups and pots
and copper vessels and dining couches. (Mark 7:3–4)

The Pharisees sometimes came into contact with unclean things
and people, which would render these religious leaders unclean.
The word for "washing" in Mark 7:4 (Gk. *baptisōntai*) literally
means "baptizing." So before Christ had instituted a new rite
of baptism (Matt. 28:18–20), the concept was clearly present in
Jewish thinking and practice.

We can go back to Noah's ark, which is a type of baptism
(1 Pet. 3:20–21). In Noah's time the people of God (i.e., Noah's
family) were brought safely through the waters of judgment,
which is a perfect picture of the meaning of baptism. The New
Testament also describes the Red Sea crossing as a "baptism"
(1 Cor. 10:2: "And all were baptized into Moses in the cloud
and in the sea"). The people of Israel were distinguished from
the wicked (i.e., Egypt) and were constituted as a new people
as they were led into the promised land. Not only were they
baptized, but they possessed the Holy Spirit as well (Isa. 63:11).
Later in Exodus, the priests were baptized (Ex. 40:12–14). Thus,
John's baptism was not something altogether new. In fact, faithful Israelites would have known and understood the significance
of baptism in their personal and corporate identity with God.

We could argue that the waters of baptism in the Old Testament functioned as the means by which God not only distinguished his people from the pagan world but also formed and
purified his people. Baptism has a redemptive significance, and
this rite belonged, at different stages in their history, to those
whom God was pleased to call his own.

When Jesus was baptized by John, then, he was not only
receiving his ordination into the ministry as prophet, priest, and

king, but he was also identifying with his people in a unique way: the baptism of forgiveness would be fulfilled in Christ's life and death. In fact, Mark makes this explicit in Mark 10:38, "Jesus said to them, 'You do not know what you are asking. Are you able to drink the cup that I drink, or to be baptized with the baptism with which I am baptized?'"

As soon as John baptized Christ, his fate was sealed: Christ would die in fulfillment of the baptism he received. The flood and the Red Sea crossing represent new beginnings, which is a fitting way to understand Christ's baptism on the cross, when he was flooded by God's wrath in order to deliver us into a new realm of life in the Spirit. Pentecost proves this: Jesus poured out his Spirit from heaven (Acts 2:33) and gifted to the church his Spirit in fulfillment of John's prophecy in Mark 1:8.

The final baptism—*the* baptism—is what we commonly call "Christian baptism." This baptism is "into Christ": "Do you not know that all of us who have been baptized into Christ Jesus were baptized into his death?" (Rom. 6:3; cf. Gal. 3:27). So when Jesus received his "baptism" (death), we were with him by representation since he is our head. Our baptism represents our union with him in this harrowing experience. Just as he was brought through this baptism into new life, so shall we who believe. So we need to remember that our baptism is first and foremost representative of a corporate experience whereby we are all engrafted into the body of Christ. A baptism is not, then, simply a rite that joins us to Christ, but it is also a rite that joins us to each other, so that we receive such blessings as new brothers, sisters, fathers, mothers, children.

Still, we must be careful not to conclude that baptism is a guarantee that we will be savingly joined to Christ. It is possible to be part of God's covenant community, enjoying certain spiritual blessings and yet rejecting them, evidence not that we lose our salvation but that we never truly possessed it. Concerning professing believers who apostatize, R. Fowler White notes that they "suffer real losses, but the losses they suffer do not include blessings they never actually had, namely, saving graces that flow from the decree of election."[2] This is the only way to make sense of the possibility of being "cut off" from the new covenant community (Rom. 11:20–24). Likewise, this spiritual yet nonsalvific loss allows us to comprehend the threatenings set forth in Hebrews 6:4–6 (see also 10:29; 12:25–29):

> For it is impossible, in the case of those who have once been enlightened, who have tasted the heavenly gift, and have shared in the Holy Spirit, and have tasted the goodness of the word of God and the powers of the age to come, and then have fallen away, to restore them again to repentance, since they are crucifying once again the Son of God to their own harm and holding him up to contempt.

So if we reject Christ after receiving the waters of baptism symbolizing salvation in him, we trample on this representation and invite on ourselves that harrowing experience delivered by the one baptized who in turn baptizes with "fire," to burn up the chaff (Luke 3:16–17). At the end of the day, the applied waters of baptism must be verified by saving faith (1 Pet. 3:20–22—so baptism is rightly noted as the water that "saves" through "the pledge of a clear conscience" [NIV] or "the answer of a good conscience" [NKJV]) in order to be waters of deliverance, as they were for Noah and his family. Otherwise, they remain for us waters symbolizing the fire of judgment. The water of baptism is a mark that Christ either was judged for us ("overwhelm[ed]," as with the waters of the flood, Ps. 88:7) or will act as a judge against us.

In summary, baptism may be understood as the following:

1. A visible sign that we belong to Christ and God since we are baptized into the name of the Father, Son, and Holy Spirit—a sign representing union with Christ that is thus a naming ceremony (Matt. 28:19; Rom. 6:3–5; Gal. 3:27)

2. A visible sign that publicly adds us to the church: "So those who received his word were baptized, and there were added that day about three thousand souls" (Acts 2:41)

3. A visible sign of cleansing from sin, or a washing: "And now why do you wait? Rise and be baptized and wash away your sins, calling on his name" (Acts 22:16; cf. Acts 2:38; 1 Cor. 6:11)

4. A visible sign of the righteousness that we have by faith—not a sign of our faith but rather a sign that our faith looks to, since it represents Christ's death and resurrection and all that those realities mean (Acts 16:30–34; Rom. 6:3; cf. Rom. 4:11)

5. A visible sign that we are not our own but belong to Christ and thus are to serve him by faith, based on God's promises to us (Rom. 6:1–11)

6. A visible sign of both salvation and judgment that awaits fulfillment in the person baptized, with Jesus facing "baptism" judgment either for us or against us, as, in the latter case, the one who baptizes "with fire" (1 Pet. 3:20–22; cf. Luke 3:16–17, 21–22; 12:50)

God's people, who are baptized, must, by faith, look to their baptism as they would look to Christ. We look to Christ as the one who washed us from our sins; looking to our baptism is the same thing.

A Visual Washing[3]

Christians have not agreed on the proper mode of baptism. Many godly Christians hold that the only proper way to baptize someone is by the full submersion of the body under water. Others allow for various modes, so long as the baptism is performed in the context of the church and in the name of the triune God.

We can all agree that baptism is a washing with water (1 Cor. 6:11; Eph. 5:26; Heb. 10:22). This washing represents our cleansing by the blood of Christ. The way in which we wash could allow for some degree of latitude on the amount of water used. The Scriptures speak of complete cleansing in terms of just the feet being washed (John 13:10), of only the hands being washed (Mark 7:2), or of a person being "sprinkled" (Ezek. 36:25). Thus, according to B. B. Warfield,

> It is not the amount of water which we employ but the purpose for which we employ it that is of [significance]. In Jesus Christ we are washed clean of all our sins. He has given us a sign that our sins are washed away and a pledge that we shall be clean in him. Any application of water which will symbolize this cleansing will serve as such a sign and seal.[4]

This, I think, is the main way we are to understand baptism: a washing of our sins.

Warfield, therefore, may have been right to say, "He who goes to the N[ew] T[estament] in hope of obtaining exact information on how to baptize, is doomed to quick disappointment. And he who affirms any particular way of baptizing, that it, and it alone, is valid baptism, has an immense burden of proof resting on his shoulders."[5] Should we not exercise some moderation and humility in an area where the New Testament seems to demand for such?

The symbolism of baptism in relation to the work of the Holy Spirit is also important for our doctrine of baptism. In both the Old and New Testaments, the Spirit is spoken of frequently in terms of sprinkling or pouring (Isa. 32:15; 44:3; Ezek. 39:29; Joel 2:28–29; Zech. 12:10; Acts 2:33; 10:44–45; cf. Isa. 52:15; Ezek. 36:25). The words "You will be baptized with the Holy Spirit" (Acts 1:5; cf. Matt. 3:11) reflect the pouring of the Spirit (Gk. *ekcheo*, Acts 2:17, 33; cf. Rom. 5:5). Whether one pours, sprinkles, or immerses, one can see how the flowing of water offers a picture of the Spirit being poured out on his people.

Jesus baptizes us with the Holy Spirit, the living water from the heavenly places, as he applies his cleansing blood to us. We now have access to the heavenly sanctuary (Heb. 10:19–22). Moreover, the baptism Christ undergoes is his death on the cross, where the wrath of God was poured out on him like a flood (Ps. 88:7; Isa. 51:17, 22; Luke 22:42). When we are baptized, we have a symbol of God's waters of judgment passing over us as we are delivered into the realm of salvation through Christ's death. One can see how either pouring or immersion can capture this truth.

Practical Benefits of Baptism

No one has ever looked forward to his or her baptism like Christ did. In Mark's account of Christ's baptism, he uses a mere fifty-three words in the original Greek, but the significance of Christ's baptism far outweighs the number of words given to the account. In Mark's account the emphasis is more on what God does to and for Jesus than on what Jesus does for God. The dawning of the kingdom of God was associated in Jewish tradition with the heavens opening, the Spirit descending, and a voice from heaven speaking. Christ's baptism contains these elements, with the undeniable focus on the fact that the Messiah is here, vindicated from on high by Yahweh.

Jesus is baptized by John (Mark 1:9), and Matthew tells us that Jesus told John why it was necessary for him to be baptized by John (Matt. 3:14–15). Israelites had prayed and hoped that God would tear open the heavens and come down (Isa. 64:1). God "comes down" in multiple ways: the incarnation, the sending of the Spirit, and the voice of the Father. The voice of the Father is key for our own understanding of the significance of our baptism. Only at Jesus's baptism (and in John 12:28) do we read of God speaking audibly to his Son. Jesus is the fulfillment of true sonship that Israel ultimately never fulfilled (see Ex. 4:22–23).

For Jesus, his baptism is an immensely significant moment in his messianic call. God affirms his love for Jesus. But his baptism means that his death is certain: he will be baptized again! Later in Mark, when Jesus's disciples ask for future glory, he affirms, "You do not know what you are asking. Are you able to drink the cup that I drink, or to be baptized with the baptism with which I am baptized?" (Mark 10:38). The fulfillment of Christ's baptism in the Jordan takes place at Calvary. At Calvary, the heavens are shut, and there is no voice. Christ's identification with sinful humanity is complete. It is true, never was God more happy to say, "This is my Son, whom I love; with him I am well pleased" (Matt. 3:17 NIV), than when Jesus was on the cross. But from Christ's perspective, there was only silence and darkness.

What does this mean for us? First, we should remember that as soon as Jesus is baptized, he is driven into the wilderness to do battle against the devil and wild animals. He was sent to suffer and be tempted. God loved Jesus and had a wonderful plan for his life! Yet that plan was not to avoid suffering but to enter into a life of suffering as the baptized Son of God. Second, Christ did not sin, because he had embraced the words of his baptism, namely, that he is God's Son. The devil tempted Jesus to throw himself down if he was God's Son. But Jesus did not need to tempt God. He only had to believe the words formerly spoken to him from the heavens. He had to live by faith and trust that what God said to him at his baptism was true. Likewise, when we are tempted, we must by faith embrace our baptism and believe that we are God's children, whom he loves. This is one way we can use our baptism to our immense benefit: to believe God's promises.

A young Christian man sitting at a computer, tempted to look at pornography, needs to remember that he has been baptized; he needs to remember he is God's child; he needs to look not at the naked women but at the God who says, "You are my child, whom I love." We have no shortage of weapons in our arsenal; we only forget to use them in our battles.

The Westminster Larger Catechism (q. 167) asks, "How is our baptism to be improved by us?" The divines note that improving on our baptism is needful but "much neglected." Yet we are to improve on our baptism by making use of our baptism "in the time of temptation" (as Christ no doubt did). Our baptism should constantly remind us of our "sinful defilement," but it should also therefore remind us to draw strength from Christ's death and resurrection so that we can mortify sin and better endeavor to live by faith as we live in love toward our neighbor as members of the body of Christ.

In other words, don't waste your baptism.

16

Fed

Some have referred to the Lord's Supper as an earthly encounter with the heavenly Christ, but I prefer to think of it as a heavenly encounter (by faith) with the heavenly Christ. All true worship takes place in heaven, which means when we eat and drink, we are doing so with a far greater "audience" than we can imagine.

Stephen Charnock says of the Lord's Supper,

> There is in this action more communion with God . . . than in any other religious act. . . . We have not so near a communion with a person, either by petitioning for something we want, or returning him thanks for a favor received, as we have by sitting with him at his table, partaking of the same bread and the same cup.[1]

He further explains,

> Christ is really presented to us, and faith really takes him, closes with him, lodges him in the soul, makes him an indweller; and the soul hath spiritual communion with him in

> his life and death, as if we did really eat his flesh and drink
> his blood presented to us in the elements.[2]

This is a basic understanding of what takes place at the Table of the Lord.

We perhaps do not get as much out of the Lord's Supper as we should because we are not well versed in the meaning of the Supper and what is actually taking place. We can debate the frequency of the Lord's Supper (e.g., weekly, monthly, or yearly?), but if we do not actually understand the significance of the Supper, then we might as well not do it at all. It may be that a fresh understanding of what it means to "eat" and "drink" will stir up a desire in us to celebrate Communion more often than perhaps we do.

Biblical Context

Here is Mark's narrative of the Lord's Supper:

> And as they were eating, he took bread, and after blessing it broke it and gave it to them, and said, "Take; this is my body." And he took a cup, and when he had given thanks he gave it to them, and they all drank of it. And he said to them, "This is my blood of the covenant, which is poured out for many. Truly, I say to you, I will not drink again of the fruit of the vine until that day when I drink it new in the kingdom of God." (Mark 14:22–25; cf. Matt. 26:26–29; Luke 22:18–20; 1 Cor. 11:23–25)

Jesus enjoys a Passover meal with his disciples, which, for Jews at that time, was a fellowship meal of rejoicing. The Jewish people remember God's mercy to those whose houses were marked with the blood of the paschal lamb. But they also anticipated God's future deliverance at this meal of celebration. But in the context of Jesus and the twelve, who represent the new people of God, the particular meal they enjoyed was a final meal with Jesus, who offered revelation that would have no doubt shocked them.

Luke informs us that Jesus reclined at table with the twelve and said to them, "I have earnestly desired to eat this Passover with you before I suffer. For I tell you I will not eat it until it is fulfilled in the kingdom of God" (Luke 22:15–16). Here at the institution of the Lord's Supper, Jesus wanted to drive home to his disciples—and indeed to himself—what was about to happen. All this makes sense when we think of the words Jesus used regarding the bread and the wine: "This is my [sacrificial] body," and "This is my [sacrificial] blood" (Mark 14:22, 24). Jesus is the Paschal Lamb, the antitype to the types. As Joachim Jeremias states,

> We have a double simile of Jesus here, which has its formal analogy in the manner in which prophets of the Old Covenant announce future events parabolically (Ezek. 4:1–17; 5:1–17; Jer. 19:1–15). Its meaning is quite simple. Each one of the disciples could understand it. Jesus made the broken bread a simile of the fate of his body, the blood of the grapes a simile of his outpoured blood.[3]

As the Paschal Lamb, Jesus uses language with his disciples to show them that his death is a saving death, not just some unfortunate circumstance of an impending trial gone wrong. His words show them, in one respect, that he is in complete control of the situation, because, ultimately, his Father is in control (Acts 2:23; 4:28). Jesus could give no greater gift to his disciples at this time than the gift of salvation, of the washing of their sins. And Yahweh was also involved in the death of the Messiah, so that his death was not to be viewed as a defeat but as a victory.

Remembrance

Luke 22:19 records that when Jesus "took bread, and when he had given thanks, he broke it and gave it to them, saying, 'This is my body, which is given for you. Do this in remembrance of me'" (see also 1 Cor. 11:24–25).

We typically think of the act of remembrance in terms of how we are to remember Christ's death. This may not actually be exclusively what Jesus had in mind. If we look at the Palestinian background of Christ's time, including various prayers that speak of God in relation to the Messiah, we may wish to understand the "remembrance" language as *God* remembering the Messiah, not just *us* remembering the Messiah. We celebrate the Lord's Supper so that God may remember Christ's work on our behalf. When the Lord's Supper is placed before the people of God, we are not the only ones remembering his death; we are proclaiming Christ's death in a significant way: "For as often as you eat this bread and drink the cup, you proclaim the Lord's death until he comes" (1 Cor. 11:26).

Jeremias goes as far as to say,

> The proclamation of the death of Jesus is not therefore intended to call to the remembrance of the community the event of the Passion; rather this proclamation expresses the vicarious death of Jesus as the beginning of salvation time and prays for the coming of the consummation. As often as the death of the Lord is proclaimed at the Lord's supper, and the *maranatha* rises upward, God is reminded of the unfulfilled climax of the work of salvation "until (the goal is reached, that) he comes."[4]

Jeremias may be overstating his position to make a point, but we can aim for a both-and, not an either-or, on this matter.

We should keep in mind the *dual* focus on what it means to "remember" in the Bible, as evidenced in Genesis 9:14–17. There the bow is a memorial. It reminds God of his covenant, and it reminds us that God reminds himself. Also, in Exodus 12 the blood of the covenant is presented to God by the Israelites. Thus, the Israelites are to remember the promise of God, but also, when the angels see the blood that is presented and painted, they are to remember the covenant and pass over the house.

Christ's Presence

Our Lord said to his disciples, "This is my body, which is given for you" (Luke 22:19), and also, speaking of the wine, "This cup that is poured out for you is the new covenant in my blood" (Luke 22:20). The bread and the wine *are* the body and blood of Christ. But how so?

The Lord's Supper involves, if it is to be of any use at all to our souls, communion with Christ: "The cup of blessing that we bless, is it not a participation in the blood of Christ? The bread that we break, is it not a participation in the body of Christ?" (1 Cor. 10:16).

What does "participation in the body of Christ" mean? It may have reference to the common enjoyment of something. But are we participating in Christ or in those who also take the Lord's Supper or both? Contextually, it seems obvious that we are participating in the body of Christ, including him as our head: we are eating his body and blood. Similarly, participation in the Passover meal meant participation in the benefits of the Passover sacrifice (Ex. 12:27; Deut. 16:2, 5–6; 2 Chron. 35:1, 6, 11). Christ, as our

Passover Lamb, was sacrificed for us so that we may receive the blessings of his death. One way we do this is in the eating and drinking of his body and blood. God is sealing to us his covenant promises, which are all "Yes" and "Amen" in Christ (2 Cor. 1:20).

The means by which we eat and drink Christ's body is through the Holy Spirit. The Spirit dwells in Christ and is poured out by Christ. Christ can choose to bless us in a number of ways, but he does so particularly through the word and sacraments. The sacraments are visible testimonies to Christ's person and work, so it makes sense for Christ to honor this covenant meal among God's people by granting his Spirit to us in the eating and drinking of his flesh. By faith we are strengthened spiritually by feasting on the risen Savior through the Spirit. God sets before us his Son, and we respond by "reminding" God of this memorial so that what is signified to us through faith on earth now will ultimately be brought about in the consummation when we eat and drink by sight in the world to come.

Matthew Poole (1624–1679) writes,

> When [Christ] said, "Take, eat," he means no more than that true believers should by the hand of their body take the bread, and with their bodily mouths eat it, and at the same time, by the hand and mouth of faith, receive and apply all the benefits of his blessed death and passion to their souls.[5]

As noted, this can take place only by the work of the Spirit. He descends from the hand of Christ to raise us up into the heavenly places for fellowship with Christ. After all, all true worship takes place in heaven.

The Lord's Supper represents everything Christianity should be. It emphasizes the bond between the Lord's people as we commune together with Christ. But the communion we enjoy is certainly not limited to the immediate sanctuary where we worship. Since we are lifted into the heavenly places in Christ Jesus, we are "surrounded by so great a cloud of witnesses" (Heb. 12:1) and so sit with them in heaven, where we eat together. As John Newton puts it,

> May the grace of Christ our Savior
> and the Father's boundless love,
> with the Holy Spirit's favor,
> rest upon us from above.
>
> Thus may we abide in union
> with each other and the Lord,
> and possess in sweet communion,
> joys which earth cannot afford.[6]

Here Newton incorporates several interrelated elements of the Christian life. All these can be applied to what it means to eat and drink the body and blood of Christ. Christianity is, as I say in the introduction, five things: Trinity oriented, Christ focused, Spirit energized, church inhabited, and heaven anticipated. How interesting that in the Lord's Supper we see all those realities come together. God the Father sets before us his Son, whom he did not withhold from us, and we commune with him, in the context of the church, by the Spirit, as a memorial to God to usher in our heavenly banquet, which is the end goal of our salvation (i.e., to eat with Jesus).

As we present bread and wine, we are also presenting the fruit of our labor. Our labor is itself a gift from God. God gives us grain and grapes—this is all grace. By his grace we transform the grain and grapes into bread and wine. We then present the bread and wine to the Father through the Spirit in the name of

Christ. When the Father sees the memorial, he remembers his Son, the Lord Jesus Christ. Then, by the gift of the Spirit, as we eat and drink in faith, the Father renews us in Christ, showering us with blessings in him. The Father sees us "in Christ" and says to us, "You are my children, my sons and daughters, in whom I am well pleased. Have life, eternal life!"

PART 5

THE HEAVEN-ANTICIPATED LIFE

17

The New Heavens
and New Earth

"Sir, I bless God, my heart is in heaven. I am well." These were the words Christopher Love spoke at his execution on August 22, 1651. If our heart is in heaven, we are well, but when our (resurrected) bodies are on the new earth, we will be even better.

God has set eternity in our hearts, a testimony to the fact that we are made in his image (Eccles. 3:11). Unsurprisingly, many people in various religions have spoken of a place called "heaven." Heaven occupies the thinking of so many not only because God has set eternity in our hearts but also because all men die (Heb. 9:27). We all hope for a better place, a better existence than what is here on earth. There is nothing in and of itself wrong with such a desire. But our desire for heaven, as well as our knowledge of the place, must be on God's terms. Whatever we say about those who have departed from this world, such words can have authority only if they proceed from the mouth of God, who exercises complete lordship over those who depart from this world.

The Christian faith in its basic form as living for God must be a heaven-anticipated life. In this life, with all its struggles and challenges, we are longing for something more beyond this world. We seek the everlasting life that we taste now in Christ and will enjoy in its fullest sense at death and beyond that, at the second coming of Christ. The young church at Thessalonica had this concept down; it was said of them that they "turned to God from idols to serve the living and true God, and to wait for his Son from heaven, whom he raised from the dead, Jesus who delivers us from the wrath to come" (1 Thess. 1:9–10). This is the Christian life in a nutshell, a life lived in worship of our triune God through Christ while waiting for our very Savior to return and bring us into heavenly glory. Yet Christians struggle to adequately meditate on heaven as they should. There are different reasons for this, but many have such inadequate views of heaven that one can understand why they think so infrequently of the place they will inhabit forever. Wrong views of heaven and God's future plans for this world can stunt our desires and hope for heaven.

History Is Circular

Biblical history is linear in an obvious sense, since it is history. But theologically speaking, biblical history has a certain circularity to it, insofar as God's original purposes for creation are ultimately realized through Christ. For example, in Eden, trees occupy a central place in God's purposes toward man. The tree of life and the tree of the knowledge of good and evil (Gen. 2:9) are central to God's relation toward Adam and Eve. Trees are a sign of redemption post-Eden: "He himself bore our sins in his body on the tree, that we might die to sin and live to righteousness. By his wounds you have been healed" (1 Pet. 2:24; see also

Deut. 21:22–23; Gal. 3:13). In the new Eden, trees are also a sign of redemption:

> Then the angel showed me the river of the water of life, bright as crystal, flowing from the throne of God and of the Lamb through the middle of the street of the city; also, on either side of the river, the tree of life with its twelve kinds of fruit, yielding its fruit each month. The leaves of the tree were for the healing of the nations. (Rev. 22:1–2)

The original Eden was a temple where God's presence was located. Adam was a "high priest" who was placed in the Most Holy Place and was tasked with guarding the "temple" (see Gen. 2:15; cf. Num. 3:7–8, which speaks of the priests who served and guarded the tabernacle).

In redemptive history, the cherubim were two statues positioned on either side of the ark of the covenant in the Most Holy Place; the tree of life in Eden was a model for the lampstand placed directly outside the Most Holy Place: the lampstand looked like a small, flowering tree with seven protruding branches. In fact, Israel's temple possessed a garden-like atmosphere (see 1 Kings 6:18). Moreover, the entrance to Eden was from the East (Gen. 3:24), which happened to be the direction from which one entered the tabernacle.

From what we can tell regarding Israelite history, and also the imagery of heaven in the book of Revelation, God will ultimately bring us back to the "garden of Eden," where our prophet, priest, and king (Jesus) will reign.[1]

Intermediate State

There is, however, an intermediate state between our life on earth and that in heaven. Many people think of heaven as the place where they go after death. While this is not false, the emphasis in the New Testament regarding "heaven" focuses on the renovation of this world. Notwithstanding this point, there is an intermediate state where believers go to be with the Lord after they die. Paul, speaking of the prospect of dying, says it is better by far to be with the Lord (Phil. 1:23). Stephen was able to see into "heaven": he saw the "glory of God, and Jesus. . . . And he said, 'Behold, I see the heavens opened'" (Acts 7:55–56).

Besides Stephen's testimony, Jesus assured the dying thief that he would be with him in paradise the very same day as his death (Luke 23:43). Interestingly, the Septuagint (i.e., the Greek translation of the Old Testament) uses the Median word *paridaeza*, which refers to a walled park or enclosed garden. And in Revelation 2:7 Christ makes the promise to those who overcome that he will give them the right "to eat of the tree of life, which is in the *paradise* of God." Revelation 2:7 may certainly be referring to the future new heavens and new earth, but we see that there is a type of similarity between what is promised to the dying thief (i.e., "paradise") in the intermediate state and what is promised to God's people in the renovated new heavens and new earth.

In the book of Revelation, we have further evidence that departed saints are now conscious beings who worship God. For example, in Revelation 6:9–11 we note that John describes the souls of those who had been slain. They are currently alive, retaining their identity as martyrs; they still call out to God, acting as rational beings aware of heaven and earth, desiring that God intervene in earthly affairs. Moreover, they not only ask questions and pray for judgment but also receive communication from God.

The Westminster Larger Catechism (q. 37) sets forth a helpful summary of the intermediate state and the glorious "benefits" all Christians receive at death (cf. 2 Cor. 5:8), with souls made perfect in holiness, and received into the highest heavens, where they behold the face of God in light and glory, waiting for the full redemption of their bodies, which even in death continue united to Christ, and rest in their graves as in their beds, till at the last day they be again united to their souls.

In sum, the Christian faith is lived with a longing to one day stand in the presence of our Savior and to do so in the sinless perfection that he alone provides.

As great and glorious as the intermediate state is, where God's people are received into Christ's glory, the preponderance of the biblical emphasis on heaven is related to what will happen after Christ returns and God makes all things new again.

Christ's Resurrection and Ours

Life after the intermediate state involves our resurrection bodies. Christ's resurrection proves our own resurrection. As John says, "What we will be has not yet appeared; but we know that when he appears, we shall be like him, because we shall see him as he is" (1 John 3:2). Jesus was raised not as a ghost or a phantom but as a human being: "See my hands and my feet, that it is I myself. Touch me, and see. For a spirit does not have flesh and bones as you see that I have" (Luke 24:39). Moreover, Jesus asked his disciples to come and have breakfast with him (John 21:12–15).

Our own bodily resurrection depends on Christ's. Believers on earth await the return of Christ, "who will transform our lowly body to be like his glorious body, by the power that enables him even to subject all things to himself" (Phil. 3:21). Just as the Spirit preserved, transformed, and raised Christ's body in the tomb, so he will also give life to our mortal bodies through transformation on earth (sanctification) that leads to glorification in heaven (Job 19:23–29; Rom. 8:11; 2 Cor. 4:14; 1 Thess. 4:15–18).

Jesus refers to those who have died but still live by their names, such as Abraham, Isaac, and Jacob (Matt. 8:11; see also Luke 16:25). We will retain our identity, for as soon as we are created, we become "eternal," in the sense that we will never ultimately pass out of existence but rather will pass into a different type of existence (i.e., heaven or hell). At bottom, the resurrection of our bodies and the new creation are linked together as fitting counterparts in God's grand plan to redeem (see Isa. 65:16–17; 2 Cor. 5:14–15; Col. 1:15–18).

Again, the Westminster Larger Catechism (q. 87) gives a wonderful synopsis of the resurrection of Christians when Christ, their firstfruits, returns:

> [Christians] found alive shall in a moment be changed; and the selfsame bodies of the dead which were laid in the grave, being then again united to their souls forever, shall be raised up by the power of Christ. The bodies of the just, by the Spirit of Christ, and by virtue of his resurrection as their head, shall be raised in power, spiritual, incorruptible, and made like to his glorious body.

At that time, we will with perfect bodies, free from all disease and weakness, look on our Savior face-to-face (1 Cor. 13:12). But there is yet something more to be experienced in the new heavens and new earth.

Heaven on Earth

Our Lord deserves a new creation where he can reign among his people as the glorified prophet, priest, and king. When God speaks in his word of the promise of the new heavens and new earth, we must remember that he has in mind the place where his Son will be the central figure who can rightfully claim to be the Lord of heaven.

In Isaiah God declares his purposes in language that should stimulate our faith, hope, and love: faith to believe what he has promised, hope to look forward to what is promised, and love to enjoy the one who promises. Consider these passages:

> For behold, I create new heavens
> and a new earth,
> and the former things shall not be remembered
> or come into mind.
> But be glad and rejoice forever
> in that which I create;
> for behold, I create Jerusalem to be a joy,
> and her people to be a gladness. (Isa. 65:17–18)

> For as the new heavens and the new earth
> that I make
> shall remain before me, says the LORD,
> so shall your offspring and your name remain. (Isa. 66:22)

Isaiah's language is echoed in the New Testament:

> Jesus said to them, "Truly, I say to you, in the new world, when the Son of Man will sit on his glorious throne, you who have followed me will also sit on twelve thrones, judging the twelve tribes of Israel." (Matt. 19:28)

> But according to his promise we are waiting for new heavens and a new earth in which righteousness dwells. (2 Pet. 3:13)

> Then I saw a new heaven and a new earth, for the first heaven and the first earth had passed away, and the sea was no more. (Rev. 21:1)

Like our bodies, which will be raised without losing our former identities, the new heavens and new earth will be re-created in terms of their former identity. God does not absolutely destroy and start brand-new with the world or us. He redeems both the world and us. The world and God's people anticipate the liberation of creation from its bondage to decay (Rom. 8:18–25). So we are filled with hope because of what God has promised.

The language in Scripture suggests that we have much to look forward to as human beings, not just as isolated souls. In other words, the very joys and delights that we possess on earth are a mere taste of the eternal joys and delights we will experience in the new heaven and new earth. Whatever food we now enjoy will be like a grain of dust compared to the food we will enjoy in heaven. The best wine today will be like vinegar compared to the wine of heaven. Our bodies and souls will enjoy all that God's renewed creation can possibly offer.

Of course, we should not lose sight of the fact that we will do all things to the glory of God, but we should also not get caught up in thinking about heaven as a place where we escape the physical. Far from it: God redeems body and soul, so that both may function as they were intended in the paradise of God.

The New Jerusalem

As noted above, God is not just re-creating a new earth for us to inhabit, but he is returning us to a better Eden. In Eden, a river went forth (Gen. 2:10). In the new Jerusalem in Revelation 22:1, the angel shows John "the river of the water of life." What Adam experienced in the original Eden will not compare to the experience of the saints in the eternal Eden.

Adam was forbidden from eating from the tree of life (Gen. 3:22–23). The tree of life was like a sacrament, in that a sacrament is a promise of life, and the tree of life had reference to the promise held out to Adam that he would live forever. In Revelation 22:2, John speaks of the "tree of life," whose leaves were "for the healing of the nations" (see also Ezek. 47:12). These images are clearly intended to bring our minds to Eden, but we must also remember that the new Eden—a paradisiacal city-temple—will be worldwide and not just a smaller location within the earth. All the nations of the earth will be welcomed into the new Jerusalem (Rev. 22:3). Those who are welcomed into God's paradisiacal temple will have Christ's name on their foreheads; they will also see his face (Rev. 22:4).

The sight of Christ's face is one of the chief blessings God's people receive. In this life we behold the glory of Christ by faith (2 Cor. 3:18; 5:7), but with the return of Jesus we will be immediately glorified (i.e., transformed) by his presence (1 John 3:2). We will see him as he is. This was Job's hope:

> For I know that my Redeemer lives,
>> and at the last he will stand upon the earth.
> And after my skin has been thus destroyed,
>> yet in my flesh I shall see God,
> whom I shall see for myself,
>> and my eyes shall behold, and not another.
>> My heart faints within me! (Job 19:25–27)

And David's:

> As for me, I shall behold your face in righteousness;
>> when I awake, I shall be satisfied with your likeness.
>> (Ps. 17:15)

And Isaiah's:

> Your eyes will behold the king in his beauty;
>> they will see a land that stretches afar. (Isa. 33:17)

And indeed Christ's own hope:

> Father, I desire that they also, whom you have given me, may be with me where I am, to see my glory that you have given me because you loved me before the foundation of the world. (John 17:24)

Heaven would not be heaven if Christ's face were not there to behold. What makes the new Jerusalem full of splendor and glory is the presence of Christ in a worldwide city-temple that possesses a beauty suited to the Lord of glory. Isaiah had prophesied a future glory for Jerusalem (Isa. 52:1). The new Jerusalem is a restoration of paradise (Rev. 21:6; 22:1–4, 14). Its stunning beauty results from the fact that it descends from heaven: "And I saw the holy city, new Jerusalem, coming down out of heaven from God, prepared as a bride adorned for her husband" (Rev. 21:2; see also 21:10).

Friends in Heaven, Forever

Besides seeing the face of Christ, we will see the faces of each other. The redeemed retain their individuality as persons. The French-Swiss poet J. Petit-Senn (1792–1870) remarked, "In a better world we will find our young years and our old friends."[2] We will not be alone forever but will be with people who delight us. Herman Bavinck had something perceptive to say about this reality:

> The hope of reunion on the other side of the grave is completely natural, genuinely human, and also in keeping with

Scripture. For Scripture teaches us not a naked immortality of spectral souls but the eternal life of individual persons. Regeneration does not erase individuality, personality, or character, but sanctifies it and puts it at the service of God's name. The community of believers is the new humanity that bears within itself a wide range of variety and distinction and manifests the richest diversity in unity. The joy of heaven, to be sure, first of all consists in communion with Christ but, further, in the fellowship of the blessed among themselves as well.[3]

Fellowship with God's people is a core aspect of our Christian life. The early believers in Acts devoted themselves to such "fellowship" (Acts 2:42), albeit in an imperfect manner. Christianity thrives on corporate fellowship among God's people, who all possess such wondrous qualities and gifts that we cannot wait to see how God will heighten these things in our eternal state when fellowship with each other and Christ will reach its zenith.

What we love now on earth we pray we will love more in heaven. In fact, there is an obvious connection between many things that are given to us on earth and our enjoyment of these same things in the world to come. Richard Baxter said, "I must confess, as the experience of my own soul, that the expectation of loving my friends in heaven principally kindles my love to them while on earth."[4] Heaven will be a world of unending love. Yet we must not think of the new heavens and earth as some sort of sensual paradise in which our fleshly desires reign supreme. All will be done and enjoyed to the glory of God, and in the most perfect way, we will "delight" ourselves in the Lord, who in turn fully grants to us "the desires of our heart" (Ps. 37:4), which will bring us the greatest pleasure and in the purest form.

Given the carnal desires that so easily consume us, such a state is hard to imagine. But one day, we will experience it and should in this life anticipate its arrival.

Because love will remain in heaven, unlike faith and hope, we will not be capable of sinning there. As the Scriptures make clear, "[God] will wipe away every tear from their eyes, and death shall be no more, neither shall there be mourning, nor crying, nor pain anymore, for the former things have passed away" (Rev. 21:4). When the trumpet sounds, we "will be raised imperishable" (1 Cor. 15:52), so that our new constitution will mean not only that we do not sin but also that we do not want to sin. We will permanently have our eyes on Jesus, which is how we are kept from sinning on earth. But also, we should remember that we are Christ's bride, and since we are united to him, there is no way we can ever lose our heavenly inheritance, because that would mean divorce! And God hates divorce.

The threefold source of temptation (i.e., the world, the devil, the flesh) will be gone, and we will have perfected natures that will always act in accordance with the great end of glorifying God in all that we do (1 Cor. 10:31). Oh the joy of meditating on what it will be like not to sin or to have even the slightest hint of wanting to sin! The Spirit will fill us to such a degree that we will be utterly incapable of anything but holiness, love, and joy.

In a most holy and God-glorifying manner, we will eat and drink, laugh and play, explore and learn, worship and rest, sing and dance, fellowship and create. We will experience the world and God's universe as far as our desires will take us; we will, in a manner of speaking, do whatever we want to do, because we will want only what is truly good. Heaven is not a place for disembodied human spirits playing harps but rather a place where our true humanity (body-soul) experiences all to the glory of God. Heaven will be a place that will get better and better, from perfection to even greater perfection. As Jonathan Edwards says,

> Therefore, their [i.e., the saints'] knowledge will increase to eternity; and if their knowledge, doubtless their holiness. For as they increase in the knowledge of God and of the works of God, the more they will see of his excellency; and the more they see of his excellency . . . the more will they love him; and the more they love God, the more delight and happiness . . . will they have in him.[5]

As finite humans, we will have a capacity for continual learning in glory. Do not neglect thinking of where you will be forever, learning more and more of the infinite God and his Son Jesus Christ through the power of the Spirit. Let the new earth that you will occupy excite you on this earth now. You can afford to give up a lot now because you will gain everything in eternity; you can afford not to care about the things of the world because you will inherit the world; you can stay calm about so many problems because the future glory to be revealed to us is not worthy to be compared with our present sufferings (Rom. 8:18). Christianity is heaven anticipated, focused on all that God has promised to do for us and for his Son. We are, some of us, far too comfortable in this world, in that the thought of heaven is nice but not all-consuming. For those who suffer for the sake of Christ, heaven is everything because Christ is everything.

Is it possible to imagine that heaven doesn't exist? We cannot with John Lennon do such a thing; it's not "easy if you try."[6] In fact, it's impossible for God's people to get heaven out of their hearts and minds. Instead, may this heaven-anticipated life be as true of us as it was of the Puritan Richard Sibbes, about whom Izaak Walton testified,

> Of this blest man, let this just praise be given,
> Heaven was in him, before he was in heaven.[7]

The Place of Outer Darkness

Christ spoke a great deal more about judgment and hell than he did about heaven. There may be many reasons for this. But we can say this: his work is magnified when we realize what we have been saved from. How much more do we love Christ when we realize that instead of eternal punishment, involving torment of our body-soul, we receive eternal life, involving the happiness and joy of our body-soul.

Can anyone speak truthfully on hell and not do so with grief in one's heart? It is truth seen too late, a place where there are no atheists and yet where no one loves the God they know exists. Being in the presence of God without a mediator is a horrible thing indeed.

Judgment

If we hate sin, then we should love judgment. But alas, we are sinners, and so there is very much left in us that hates the idea of judgment. But that does not mean there will be no judgment. Jesus came to earth to save (John 3:17), but he will return to judge. Judgment has always been a feature of God's activity in this world, whether with respect to those outside the church (e.g., Pharaoh, Egypt) or those inside the church (e.g., Korah, Ananias and Sapphira).

Judgment has been committed to the Son (John 5:22), so that those who fail to honor the Son will nevertheless be judged by the Son and forced to acknowledge his lordship (Phil. 2:11). At the final judgment, the wicked will be publicly convinced of their guilt, something they have denied while on earth. They will be tried according to God's standard of righteousness. Those who were impenitent on earth will have their sins rehearsed afresh so that God's sentence on them is righteous. Thankfully, David understood this before it was too late:

> Against you, you only, have I sinned
>   and done what is evil in your sight,
> so that you may be justified in your words
>   and blameless in your judgment. (Ps. 51:4)

God, through Christ, will put the wicked in their place. He did so, in part, over the course of world history (e.g., the flood, Sodom and Gomorrah), but the final judgment will be worse than what the inhabitants of Sodom and Gomorrah experienced. Christianity without a final judgment is like a house without walls. The word of God expressly declares that a final judgment will take place. In fact, it is as clear as any doctrine in the Scriptures (see Matt. 12:36–37; 13:49–50; John 5:28–29; Rom. 14:12; Heb. 9:27; Rev. 20:12).

Our Lord must judge at the final day because his glory must be manifested for all to see. He came to earth in a state of humiliation, with his godhead veiled, but when he returns definitively to execute judgment, he will come in his exaltation. When

Christ came the first time, he was subject to the false and wicked judgment of men, but when he returns, men will be subject to the true and righteous judgment of the God-man. The one who suffered publicly will publicly triumph.

Paul makes an important statement on the final judgment in his second letter to the Corinthians: "For we must all appear before the judgment seat of Christ, so that each one may receive what is due for what he has done in the body, whether good or evil" (2 Cor. 5:10). This text shows that all people, without exception, will appear before the judgment seat of Christ. Men and women, boys and girls, Jews and Gentiles, slave and free, rich and poor: all will be judged. And from among these people who are judged, Jesus "will place the sheep on his right, but the goats on the left" (Matt. 25:33).

Christians, clothed in the righteousness of Christ and indwelled by the Spirit, will be able to stand in the judgment, notwithstanding their sins done in the body both before conversion and after. But the wicked will have no "clothing of righteousness" to protect them from the righteous judgment of the one who sees and knows all thoughts and deeds.

Preachers must not be shy about Christ's role as Judge. Peter says in Acts 10:42, "And [God] commanded us to preach to the people and to testify that [Jesus] is the one appointed by God to be judge of the living and the dead." Jesus possesses this honor because of his wisdom, justice, power, and authority. No one will be unfairly judged by Christ, for he is perfectly suited to be able to judge, because of his gifts and graces as the God-man.

What do all people have to look forward to? Some have the hope of heaven; others have the prospect of punishment. But all will "see the Son of Man coming on the clouds of heaven with power and great glory" (Matt. 24:30; see also 2 Thess. 1:7–10; Rev. 19:11–16).

Eternal Punishment[1]

When we speak of heaven and hell, we should speak not in generalities but in as many specifics as the Scriptures allow, which includes those of "good and necessary consequence" (Westminster Confession of Faith 1.6; cf. Matt. 22:32). Preachers may reference the horrors of hell or the happiness of heaven in a sermon but to little effect because they fail to explain why hell will be so horrible and heaven will be so happy. The idea that hell is merely "separation from God" is misleading and wrongheaded, though it certainly includes the idea of separation from Christ (Matt. 25:41). Rather, it is the opposite: a God-hating sinner, who does not have a mediator, remains in the presence of a holy, righteous, and powerful God.

Christ spoke about the specifics of hell more than anyone else in the Bible. But he did not merely talk about hell; rather, he also described hell: "And do not fear those who kill the body but cannot kill the soul. Rather fear him who can destroy both soul and body in hell" (Matt. 10:28). The Scriptures speak specifically about eternal realities. For example, consider the language of Luke 3:17, "His winnowing fork is in his hand, to clear his threshing floor and to gather the wheat into his barn, but the chaff he will burn with unquenchable fire." Elsewhere, hell is described as a "fiery furnace," where there will be "weeping and gnashing of teeth" (Matt. 13:42; see also 8:12; 13:50; 22:13; 24:51; 25:30). Moreover, hell is a "lake of fire" (Rev. 19:20), an "eternal fire" (Jude 7), "outer darkness" (Matt. 22:13), blackness of darkness forever (Jude 13), and a place where "their worm does not die and the fire is not quenched" (Mark 9:48; see also Isa. 66:22–24).

Hell is a place, not a metaphor to describe some inner thought process. The rich man in hell calls it a "place of torment" (Luke 16:28). Judas went to "his own place" (Acts 1:25). Just as there is a "place" for the righteous after death, so there is a "place" for the wicked after death. Typically, in the New Testament, the Greek word Gehenna is used for hell (e.g., Matt. 5:22, 29, 30; 10:28; Mark 9:42, 45, 47; Luke 12:5; James 3:6). Gehenna refers to the Valley of Hinnom, outside Jerusalem. This place has a horrible history, with Israelites and kings of Israel, at one time, burning their children as sacrifices to false gods (i.e., Molech):

> And [Manasseh] burned his sons as an offering in the Valley of the Son of Hinnom, and used fortune-telling and omens and sorcery. . . . He did much evil in the sight of the LORD, provoking him to anger. (2 Chron. 33:6; Ahaz did much of the same—see 2 Chron. 28:3)

Jeremiah also notes of the wicked Israelites,

> They built the high places of Baal in the Valley of the Son of Hinnom, to offer up their sons and daughters to Molech, though I did not command them, nor did it enter into my mind, that they should do this abomination, to cause Judah to sin. (Jer. 32:35)

Gehenna may not be a reference to a burning trash dump, but it is actually far worse: a place where the most horrible things take place, such as the willful sacrifice of children. Evil at its worst is associated with Gehenna. Hell is a place of pure evil, a place as scary as it is destitute of all hope. And it is an everlasting place.

At the final judgment, Jesus will "say to those on his left, 'Depart from me, you cursed, into the eternal fire prepared for the devil and his angels'" (Matt. 25:41). The fire is eternal. Paul likewise writes in 2 Thessalonians 1:9, "They will suffer the punishment of eternal destruction, away from the presence of the Lord and from the glory of his might." In the New Testament, the same word used to describe "*everlasting* life" is also used to describe "*everlasting* punishment." Indeed, in Revelation 22:14–15 we see that the existence of the righteous in heaven is coterminous with the existence of the wicked "outside" heaven (i.e., in hell).

In connection with the language used to describe hell, Calvin made this pertinent point:

> Now, because no description can deal adequately with the gravity of God's vengeance against the wicked, their torments and tortures are figuratively expressed to us by physical things, that is, by darkness, weeping, and gnashing of teeth. . . . By such expressions the Holy Spirit certainly intended to confound all our senses with dread.[2]

A Pastoral Word

It takes a great deal of faith to believe in the doctrine of endless punishment. This is not an easy doctrine for anyone to swallow, even those who believe with all their heart in the perfect justice of an infinitely holy God. We must not deny this doctrine; we must not ignore this doctrine and so practically deny it; but we must also make sure that when we speak on hell, especially from the pulpit or from the pen, people are aware that a certain lamentation is appropriate when we speak of those in hell who have rejected Christ.

The psalmist said,

> My eyes shed streams of tears,
> because people do not keep your law. (Ps. 119:136)

How much more so should we shed streams of tears because people are going to hell? Sinclair Ferguson recounts the story of a conversation between the great Scottish preachers Robert Murray M'Cheyne and Andrew Bonar:

> When Robert M'Cheyne met his dearest friend Andrew Bonar one Monday and inquired what Bonar had preached on the previous day, only to receive the answer "Hell," he asked: "Did you preach it with tears?" That we cannot do until we have come to recognize our own great need of grace to save us from the wrath to come, the terrible nature of that judgment, the provision that God has made for us in Christ, and the calling he has given us to take the gospel to every creature in the name of the One who did not come into the world to condemn it but to save it.
>
> So we are called to preach as his representatives: with biblical balance, with a Christocentric focus, with the humility of those who realize their own need of grace before the judgment seat of Christ, with a willingness to suffer in the light of the coming glory, with love and compassion in our hearts, and in a way that commends and adorns the doctrine of God our Savior.[3]

Hell is ugly; hell is real. Sadly, people will go there because they have not loved Christ with an undying and incorruptible love (1 Cor. 16:22). It is a place full of people, yet everyone will be lonely forever. It is a foul, horrible, horrific place that has no appeal, and yet the devil makes the road to hell very attractive. The terrors are real, and the only way to avoid such terrors is to put one's faith in the person who experienced the terrors of hell on the cross.

Jesus shrieked that we might sing; he cried that we might rejoice; he was thirsty that we might drink; he was abandoned that we might have fellowship; he was crushed that we might be preserved; he was in darkness that we might live in the light; he was shamed that we might be exalted; he was mocked that we might be praised; he died that we might live. Hell is real, but it is not a necessary destination when confronted with the Savior who experienced hell's terrors to secure for us heaven's happiness.

Living to God

A Final Word

Going back to Richard Baxter in our introduction, "The common zeal for Christian Religion, is not so easie to be kindled," but it is not impossible. Recognizing our own weakness and utter dependence on a sovereign God of grace who freely saves us in our blessed Redeemer, Jesus Christ, we can, one step at a time and one day at a time, take up "living to God through Christ" in the manner noted by William Ames and Petrus van Mastricht. Live then, my brothers and sisters in Christ, a Trinity-oriented, Christ-focused, Spirit-energized, church-inhabited, and heaven-anticipated life for the glory of God and the good of your soul.

Notes

Introduction

1. C. S. Lewis, "On the Reading of Old Books," in *God in the Dock: Essays on Theology and Ethics* (Grand Rapids, MI: Eerdmans, 1970), 205.
2. William Ames, *The Marrow of Theology*, trans. and ed. John D. Eusden (1968; repr., Grand Rapids, MI: Baker, 1997), 77.
3. Petrus van Mastricht, *Theoretical-Practical Theology*, vol. 1, *Prolegomena*, ed. Joel R. Beeke, trans. Todd M. Rester (Grand Rapids, MI: Reformation Heritage Books, 2018), 98.
4. Van Mastricht, *Theoretical-Practical Theology*, 1:99.
5. Richard Baxter, *Church-History of the Government of Bishops and Their Councils Abbreviated* (London, 1680), from the section "What History Is Credible, and What Not," immediately after the preface.
6. Richard Baxter, *Now or Never*, in *The Practical Works of Richard Baxter* (London: James Duncan, 1830), 7:558.
7. Baxter, *Now or Never*, in *Practical Works*, 7:558.
8. John Owen, *The Works of John Owen*, ed. William H. Goold (London: Banner of Truth, 1967), 12:70. Biddle's denial of the preexistence of Christ showed affinity for Arianism, the founder of which is arguably Lucian (the teacher of Arius), who died more than thirteen years before the Council of Nicea in 325.
9. Francis Turretin, *Institutes of Elenctic Theology*, ed. James T. Dennison Jr., trans. George Musgrave Giger (Phillipsburg, NJ: P&R, 1992), 1.14.24.
10. Quotations from the Westminster Standards come from the original edition printed in London in 1647. I have updated the language for readability.
11. Van Mastricht, *Theoretical-Practical Theology*, 1:98.

Chapter 1

1. Monarchianism is used in connection with the ancient and heretical tendency toward a monotheistic commitment to the indivisible essence of the one God while denying distinct persons within the Godhead when speaking of the relationship between Father, Son, and Spirit. Modalistic Monarchianism sees the three as "modes" of expression for the same person, meaning that Jesus modally (not personally) manifested divinity, like a sunbeam radiating from the sun. Dynamic Monarchianism sees the three as expressions of "power" for the same person, meaning that Jesus the man was empowered or adopted (thus Adoptionism) by the Godhead in his adoption as God's Son at his baptism.

2. Fred Sanders, "Who Said 'The Trinity: Try to Understand It, and You'll Lose Your Mind'?," *The Scriptorium Daily* (blog), August 29, 2009, http://scriptoriumdaily.com/who-said-the-trinity-try-to-understand-it -and-youll-lose-your-mind/.

3. In Philip Schaff, *The Creeds of Christendom, with A History and Critical Notes* (New York: Harper, 1919), 66.

4. In his greater catechism, John Owen defined "person" as "a distinct manner of subsistence or being, distinguished from the other persons by its own properties." These distinguishing properties he gave as follows:

   • The Father is the "only fountain of the Godhead (John 5:26, 27; Eph. 1:3)."
   • The Son is "begotten of his Father from eternity (Ps. 2:7; John 1:14; 3:16)."
   • The Spirit is said "to proceed from the Father and the Son (John 14:17; 16:14; 15:26; 20:22)."

   John Owen, *The Works of John Owen*, ed. William H. Goold (London: Banner of Truth, 1967), 1:472.

5. Parts of this section are adapted from Joel R. Beeke and Mark Jones, *A Puritan Theology: Doctrine for Life* (Grand Rapids, MI: Reformation Heritage Books, 2012), 91–93. Used by permission of Reformation Heritage Books.

6. Quoted in Stephen R. Holmes, *The Quest for the Trinity: The Doctrine of God in Scripture, History and Modernity* (Downers Grove, IL: InterVarsity Press, 2012), 132.

7. Gregory of Nazianzus, *Orations*, 40.41, as quoted in Robert Letham, *The Holy Trinity: In Scripture, History, Theology, and Worship* (Phillipsburg, NJ: P&R, 2004), 378.

8. This is so in a metaphorical sense, not in the modalistic sense of a sunbeam described in the introduction.

9. Charles Hodge, *Systematic Theology*, 3 vols. (Grand Rapids, MI: Eerdmans, 1968), 1:443.

10. Owen further states,

> The sum of it is: That God is one—his nature or his being one: that all the properties or infinite essential excellencies of God, as God, do belong to that one nature and being: that this God is infinitely good, holy, just, powerful; he is eternal, omnipotent, omnipresent; and these things belong to none but him—that is, that one God: that this God is the Father, Son, and Holy Ghost; which are not diverse names of the same person, nor distinct attributes or properties of the same nature or being, but one, another, and a third, all equally that one God, yet really distinguished between themselves by such incommunicable properties as constitute the one to be that one, and the other to be that other, and the third to be that third.

Owen, *Works*, 16:340.

11. Owen, *Works*, 16:339–41.

Chapter 2

1. Parts of this section are adapted from Mark Jones, "Worship," *Tabletalk*, November 1, 2011, https://www.ligonier.org/learn/articles/worship/. Used by permission of *Tabletalk*.

2. John Piper, *Let the Nations Be Glad! The Supremacy of God in Missions*, 2nd ed. (Leicester, UK: Inter-Varsity Press, 2003), 17.

3. Augustine, *On Christian Doctrine*, ed. Marcus Dods (Edinburgh: T&T Clark, 1892), 10 (1.5).

4. J. I. Packer, *A Quest for Godliness: The Puritan Vision of the Christian Life* (Wheaton, IL: Crossway, 1990), 204.

5. Thomas Goodwin, *The Works of Thomas Goodwin* (Grand Rapids, MI: Reformation Heritage Books, 2006), 8:378–79.

6. As for the Spirit as "legal counselor," John Owen writes,

> The soul, by the power of its own conscience, is brought before the law of God. There a man puts in his plea, that he is a child of God, that he belongs to God's family; and for this end produces all his evidences, every thing whereby faith gives him an interest in God. Satan, in the meantime, opposes with all his might; sin and law assist him; many flaws are found in his evidences; the truth of them all is

questioned; and the soul hangs in suspense as to the issue. In the midst of the plea and contest the Comforter comes, and, by a word of promise or otherwise, overpowers the heart with a comfortable persuasion (and bears down all objections) that his plea is good, and that he is a child of God. . . . When our spirits are pleading their right and title, he comes in and bears witness on our side; at the same time enabling us to put forth acts of filial obedience, kind and child-like; which is called "crying, Abba, Father" (Gal. 4:6).

John Owen, *The Works of John Owen*, ed. William H. Goold (London: Banner of Truth, 1967), 2:241.

7. Modified from John Owen, *Communion with God*, in Owen, *Works*, 2:236–49.

8. Owen, "A Practical Exposition upon Psalm CXXX," in *Works*, 6:459.

Chapter 3

1. Quoted in Maturin M. Ballou, *Edge-Tools of Speech* (Boston: Ticknor, 1886), 497.

2. Quoted in Geo. C. Needham, ed., *The Life and Labors of Charles H. Spurgeon* (Boston: D. L. Guernsey, 1883), 439.

3. Augustine, *The Confessions*, trans. Maria Boulding, ed. John E. Rotelle, vol. 1 of *The Works of Saint Augustine: A Translation for the 21st Century* (Hyde Park, NY: New City Press, 1997), 1.1.

4. John Calvin, *Commentary upon the Acts of the Apostles*, ed. Henry Beveridge (Edinburgh: Calvin Translation Society, 1844), 276.

5. This idea, found in many sermons (e.g., by Thomas Watson [1620–1686]) and books on theology (e.g., by Nicholas of Cusa [1401–1464]), comes from *The Book of 24 Philosophers*. See *Liber Viginti Quattuor Philosophorum*, ed. Francoise Hudry, Hermes Latinus 3.1, Corpus Christianorum, Continuatio Mediaevalis 143A (Turnhout, Belgium: Brepols, 1997), 1: "Deus est sphaera infinita cuius centrum est ubique, circumferentia nusquam."

6. Augustine, *Confessions*, 1.4.

7. Augustine, *Confessions*, 1.4.

8. Anselm of Canterbury, *Proslogium*, in Phillip Campbell, *The Catholic Middle Ages: Primary Document Catholic Study Course* (Grass Lake, MI: Cruachan Hill Press, 2016), 60; language modernized.

Chapter 4

1. J. C. Shairp, *Culture and Religion in Some of Their Relations* (New York: Hurd & Houghton, 1871), 144.

2. George Herbert, *Herbert's Poems* (London: W. Baynes and Son, 1824), 159.

3. Augustine, *Sermons 184–229*, trans. Edmund Hill, ed. John E. Rotelle, vol. 6 of *The Works of Saint Augustine: A Translation for the 21st Century* (Hyde Park, NY: New City Press, 1993), 191.1.

Chapter 5

1. John Calvin, *Institutes of the Christian Religion*, ed. John T. McNeill, trans. Ford Lewis Battles (Louisville: Westminster John Knox, 2008), 2.16.1.

2. John Owen writes, "The incarnate Son of God in His glorified humanity will be the mediator of the saints' knowledge and love for the triune God." He continues,

> All communications from the Divine Being and infinite fullness in heaven unto the glorified saints, are in and through Christ Jesus, who shall forever be the medium of communication between God and the church, even in glory. All things being gathered into one head in him, even things in heaven and things in earth, . . . this order shall never be dissolved. . . . And on these communications from God through Christ depend entirely our continuance in a state of blessedness and glory.

John Owen, *Meditations and Discourses on the Glory of Christ*, in *The Works of John Owen, D.D.* (Edinburgh: Johnstone & Hunter, 1850–1855), 1:414.

3. Richard Sibbes, *Christ's Exaltation Purchased by Humiliation*, in *The Complete Works of Richard Sibbes*, ed. Alexander B. Grosart (Edinburgh: James Nichol, 1863), 5:346.

Chapter 6

1. Stephen Charnock, *The Complete Works of Stephen Charnock* (1864–1866; repr., Edinburgh: Banner of Truth, 1985), 3:519.

2. In this section I was especially helped by the thoughts of John Owen, *The Works of John Owen*, ed. William H. Goold (London: Banner of Truth, 1967), 2:155–65. In this chapter I focus on Christ's lifelong obedience and his suffering on the cross. In the chapter on Christ's office (chap. 5), I look at his intercessory work as priest.

3. Owen, *Works*, 2:156.

4. Owen, *Works*, 2:157.

5. John Murray, *Redemption Accomplished and Applied* (Grand Rapids, MI: Eerdmans, 1955), 21.

6. Murray, *Redemption Accomplished and Applied*, 21. John Owen makes his own similar point regarding Christ's obedient suffering:

> That which we plead is, *that the Lord Christ fulfilled the whole law for us*; he did not only undergo the penalty of it due unto our sins, but also yielded that perfect obedience which it did require. And herein I shall not immix myself in the debate of the distinction between the active and passive obedience of Christ; for he exercised the highest active obedience in his suffering, when he offered himself to God through the eternal Spirit. And all his obedience, considering his person, was mixed with suffering, as a part of his . . . humiliation; whence it is said, that "though he were a Son, yet learned he obedience by the things which he suffered." And however doing and suffering are in various categories of things, yet Scripture testimonies are not to be regulated by philosophical artifices and terms. And it must needs be said, that the sufferings of Christ, as they were purely penal, are imperfectly called his passive righteousness; for all righteousness is either in *habit* or in *action*, whereof suffering is neither; nor is any man righteous, or so esteemed, from what he suffers. Neither do sufferings give satisfaction unto the commands of the law, which require only obedience. And hence it will unavoidably follow, that we have need of more than the mere sufferings of Christ, whereby we may be justified before God, if so be that any righteousness be required thereunto; but the whole of what I intend is, *that Christ's fulfilling of the law, in obedience unto its commands, is no less imputed unto us for our justification than his undergoing the penalty of it is.*

Owen, *Works*, 5:253–55; emphasis added.

7. John Calvin, *Institutes of the Christian Religion*, ed. John T. McNeill, trans. Ford Lewis Battles (Louisville: Westminster John Knox, 2008), 2.16.5.

8. Quoted in Charnock, *Works*, 4:518.

9. Similarly, John Owen writes, "A sacrifice is a religious oblation, wherein something by the ministry of a priest, appointed of God thereunto, is dedicated to God, and destroyed as to what it was, for the ends and purposes of spiritual worship whereunto it is instituted." Owen, *Works*, 12:431.

10. See Owen, *Works*, 12:431.

11. H. Richard Niebuhr, *The Kingdom of God in America* (Middletown, CT: Wesleyan University Press, 1988), 193.

Chapter 7

1. Gregory of Nazianzus, *A Select Library of Nicene and Post-Nicene Fathers of the Christian Church*, 2nd ser., ed. Philip Schaff and Henry Wace (New York: Christian Literature Company, 1894), 7:426.
2. J. Gresham Machen, *Christianity and Liberalism* (1923; repr., Grand Rapids, MI: Eerdmans, 1977), 28–29.
3. John Owen, *The Works of John Owen*, ed. William H. Goold (London: Banner of Truth, 1967), 1:263–64; emphasis added.
4. Thomas Watson, *A Body of Divinity* (1692; repr., Edinburgh: Banner of Truth, 1978), 205.
5. Watson, *Body of Divinity*, 205–6.

Chapter 8

1. Moncure Daniel Conway, ed., *The Sacred Anthology: A Book of Ethnical Scriptures*, 5th ed. (London: Trubner & Co., 1876), 235.
2. John Calvin, *Institutes of the Christian Religion*, ed. John T. McNeill, trans. Ford Lewis Battles (Louisville: Westminster John Knox, 2008), 3.1.1.
3. Calvin, *Institutes of the Christian Religion*, 3.1.1.
4. Reformed theologians in the seventeenth century typically spoke of a threefold union with Christ, in terms of God's immanent, transient, and applicatory union. *Immanent union* refers to being elected in union with Christ from all eternity, "before the foundation of the world" (Eph. 1:4); *transient union* refers to believers' union with Christ in time past, in his mediatorial death and resurrection (Rom. 6:3–11); and *applicatory union* refers to the believer's experience of union with Christ in the present (Eph. 2:5–6).
5. Herman Witsius, *Conciliatory, or Irenical Animadversions on the Controversies Agitated in Britain, under the Unhappy Names of Antinomians and Neonomians*, trans. Thomas Bell (Glasgow: W. Lang, 1807), 68.
6. Thomas Goodwin, *The Works of Thomas Goodwin* (Grand Rapids, MI: Reformation Heritage Books, 2006), 5:350.
7. Goodwin, *Works*, 5:350.
8. B. B. Warfield, *Studies in Theology* (Edinburgh: Banner of Truth, 1988), 314.
9. John Calvin, *Commentary on the First Epistle of Paul the Apostle to the Corinthians*, trans. John Fraser, Calvin's New Testament Commentaries 9 (Grand Rapids, MI: Eerdmans, 1969), comm. on 1 Cor. 1:5.

10. Abraham Kuyper, *The Work of the Holy Spirit*, trans. Henri De Vries (New York: Cosimo Classics, 2007), 461.
11. Sinclair Ferguson, *The Holy Spirit* (Downers Grove, IL: InterVarsity Press, 1996), 72. See also Kuyper, *Work of the Holy Spirit*, 461.

Chapter 9

1. J. K. Hoyt, *The Cyclopedia of Practical Quotations* (New York: Funk and Wagnalls, 1896), 706.
2. Thomas Goodwin, *The Works of Thomas Goodwin* (Grand Rapids, MI: Reformation Heritage Books, 2006), 6:3.
3. John Owen, *The Works of John Owen*, ed. William H. Goold (London: Banner of Truth, 1967), 3:23.
4. Sinclair Ferguson, *The Holy Spirit* (Downers Grove, IL: InterVarsity Press, 1996), 55.
5. Ferguson, *The Holy Spirit*, 55–56.
6. Parts of this section are adapted from Joel R. Beeke and Mark Jones, *A Puritan Theology: Doctrine for Life* (Grand Rapids, MI: Reformation Heritage Books, 2012), 469–70. Used by permission of Reformation Heritage Books.
7. William Whately, *The New Birth* (London, 1622), 13.
8. Peter van Mastricht, *A Treatise on Regeneration* (Morgan, PA: Soli Deo Gloria, 2002), 36.
9. John Flavel, *The Method of Grace*, in *The Works of John Flavel* (1820; repr., Edinburgh: Banner of Truth, 1997), 2:96–98.
10. Augustus Toplady, "A Debtor to Mercy Alone," 1771; emphasis added.

Chapter 10

1. John Calvin, *Institutes of the Christian Religion*, ed. John T. McNeill, trans. Ford Lewis Battles (Louisville: Westminster John Knox, 2008), 1.1.1.
2. Ralph Venning, *Sin, the Plague of Plagues, or, Sinful Sin the Worst of Evils . . .* (London, 1669), 225–26.
3. J. I. Packer, *Rediscovering Holiness: Know the Fullness of Life with God* (Ventura, CA: Regal, 2009), 99.
4. The words of the final Greek clause of Rom. 5:12 (*eph' hō pantes hēmarton*) can be translated as a causal clause, "for that all have sinned" (KJV), or as a simple relative clause, "in whom all have sinned" (KJV margin note). The latter rendering reflects the Latin Vulgate (*in quo omnes peccaverunt*). Those denying the immediate imputation of Adam's guilt prefer the causal rendering, "in that all have sinned." Even if one takes *eph' hō* as "in that," that is, as introducing a causal clause, we can still say that it implies that all have sinned and are

therefore guilty because of an act of sinning. Likewise, Francis Turretin argues that "whatever way *eph' hō* is translated, whether relatively, 'in whom,' . . . or causally, it amounts to the same thing." Francis Turretin, *Institutes of Elenctic Theology*, ed. James T. Dennison Jr., trans. George Musgrave Giger (Phillipsburg, NJ: P&R, 1992), 9.9.17. This note is adapted from Joel R. Beeke and Mark Jones, *A Puritan Theology: Doctrine for Life* (Grand Rapids, MI: Reformation Heritage Books, 2012), 206–7. Used by permission of Reformation Heritage Books.

5. Martin Luther, "Ninety-Five Theses," in *Career of the Reformer I*, ed. Harold J. Grimm, vol. 31 of *Luther's Works*, ed. Jaroslav Pelikan and Helmut T. Lehmann, American ed. (Philadelphia: Fortress, 1957), 25.

6. John Milton, *The Poetical Works of John Milton*, ed. Sir Egerton Brydges (London: William Tegg, 1853), 538.

7. E.g., Thomas Brooks, *The Select Works of the Rev. Thomas Brooks* (London: L. B. Seeley and Son, 1824), 1:335; Thomas Watson, *A Body of Divinity* (Glasgow: William Paton, 1794), 570.

Chapter 11

1. J. C. Ryle, *Holiness: Its Nature, Hindrances, Difficulties, and Roots* (Chicago: Moody Publishers, 2010), 80.

2. Martin Luther, *A Commentary upon the Epistle of Paul the Apostle to the Galatians* (Philadelphia: R. Aitken, 1801), 140.

3. John Owen, *The Works of John Owen*, ed. William H. Goold (London: Banner of Truth, 1967), 5:163.

4. Owen, *Works*, 3:519.

5. Thomas Goodwin, *The Works of Thomas Goodwin* (Grand Rapids, MI: Reformation Heritage Books, 2006), 1:82.

6. Goodwin, *Works*, 1:82.

7. Owen, *Works*, 6:7.

8. "Be Thou My Vision," trans. Mary Elizabeth Byrne, versified by Eleanor H. Hall, from an ancient Irish poem often attributed to Dallán Forgaill, ca. 6th century.

Chapter 12

1. Saint Anselm, *Proslogium*, trans. S. N. Deane, 2nd ed. (La Salle, IL: Open Court, 1962), 7.

2. Parts of this section are adapted from Joel R. Beeke and Mark Jones, *A Puritan Theology: Doctrine for Life* (Grand Rapids, MI: Reformation Heritage Books, 2012), 19, 22. Used by permission of Reformation Heritage Books.

3. John Calvin, *Institutes of the Christian Religion*, ed. John T. McNeill, trans. Ford Lewis Battles (Louisville: Westminster John Knox, 2008), 1.9.3.

4. Calvin, *Institutes*, 1.9.3.

5. John Owen, *The Works of John Owen*, ed. William H. Goold (London: Banner of Truth, 1967), 4:12.

6. Owen, *Works*, 16:320.

7. Owen, *Works*, 16:322.

8. Owen, *Works*, 16:324–25.

9. Thomas Goodwin, *The Works of Thomas Goodwin* (Grand Rapids, MI: Reformation Heritage Books, 2006), 1:290.

10. Second Helvetic Confession, in *Creeds of the Churches: A Reader in Christian Doctrine from the Bible to the Present*, ed. John H. Leith, 3rd ed. (Louisville: Westminster John Knox, 1982), 133.

11. Parts of this section are adapted from Mark Jones, "The Death of Prayer Meetings," *Reformation21* (blog), Alliance of Confessing Evangelicals, May 11, 2015, http://www.reformation21.org/blog/2015/05/the-problem-of-corporate-praye.php. Used by permission of the Alliance of Confessing Evangelicals.

12. John Bunyan, "On Praying in the Spirit," in *The Works of John Bunyan* (London: Blackie and Son, 1862), 1:631.

13. Thomas Shepard, *The Works of Thomas Shepard* (Boston: Doctrinal Tract & Book Society, 1853), 2:245.

14. Henry Scudder, *A Key of Heaven: The Lord's Prayer Opened . . .* (London, 1633), 56.

15. Owen, *Works*, 3:193.

16. Richard Sibbes, *The Complete Works of Richard Sibbes*, ed. Alexander B. Grossart (Edinburgh: James Nichol, 1863), 4:208.

Chapter 13

1. Cyprian, *Treatise on the Unity of the Church*, in vol. 5 of *The Ante-Nicene Fathers*, ed. Alexander Roberts and James Donaldson (New York: Charles Scribner's Sons, 1908), 423.

2. John Calvin, *Institutes of the Christian Religion*, ed. John T. McNeill, trans. Ford Lewis Battles (Louisville: Westminster John Knox, 2008), 4.1.1.

3. Edmund P. Clowney, *The Church*, Contours of Christian Theology (Downers Grove, IL: InterVarsity Press, 1995), 31.

4. Some material in this section previously appeared in Mark Jones, "Why You Should Be a Presbyterian," The Gospel Coalition, December 12, 2013, https://www.thegospelcoalition.org/article/why-you-should-be-a-presbyterian/.

5. Thomas Peck, *Notes on Ecclesiology* (Richmond, VA: Presbyterian Committee of Publication, 1892), 205.
6. Guy Prentiss Waters, *How Jesus Runs the Church* (Phillipsburg, NJ: P&R, 2011), 23.
7. See the Belgic Confession (1561), art. 28: "We believe that since this holy assembly and congregation is the gathering of those who are saved and *there is no salvation apart from it,* no one ought to withdraw from it, content to be by himself, regardless of his status or condition." "The Belgic Confession," Reformed Church in America, accessed July 11, 2019, https://www.rca.org/resources/belgic-confession-article-28 -obligations-church-members. And see the Westminster Confession of Faith 25.2, "The visible church, which is also catholic or universal under the gospel (not confined to one nation, as before under the law), consists of all those throughout the world that profess the true religion; and of their children: and is the kingdom of the Lord Jesus Christ, the house and family of God, *out of which there is no ordinary possibility of salvation.*"

Chapter 14

1. The Westminster Confession of Faith 1.6 states,

> Nevertheless we acknowledge the inward illumination of the Spirit of God to be necessary for the saving under-standing of such things as are revealed in the Word; and that there are some circumstances concerning the worship of God, and the government of the Church, common to human actions and societies, which are to be ordered by the light of nature and Christian prudence, according to the general rules of the Word, which are always to be observed.

2. Reginald Heber, "Holy, Holy, Holy," 1826.
3. Anonymous, "Come, Thou Almighty King," ca. 1757.
4. This and the following paragraph are adapted from Mark Jones, "Why Christians Must Sing Hymns," Calvinist International, June 1, 2017, https://calvinistinternational.com/2017/06/01/christians-must-sing -hymns/. Used by permission of the Calvinist International.

Chapter 15

1. Quoted in Heiko A. Oberman, *Luther: Man between God and the Devil* (New Haven, CT: Yale University Press, 2006), 105.
2. R. Fowler White, "Covenant and Apostasy," in *The Auburn Avenue Theology, Pros and Cons: Debating the Federal Vision*, ed. E. Calvin Beisner (Fort Lauderdale, FL: Knox Theological Seminary, 2003), 214.

3. Parts of this section are adapted from Mark Jones, "The Mode and Meaning of Baptism," Calvinist International, September 28, 2018, https://calvinistinternational.com/2018/09/24/the-mode-and-meaning -of-baptism/. Used by permission of the Calvinist International.

4. Benjamin B. Warfield, *Selected Shorter Writings of Benjamin B. Warfield* (Phillipsburg, NJ: P&R, 1970), 1:329.

5. Warfield, *Selected Shorter Writings*, 2:335.

Chapter 16

1. Stephen Charnock, "A Discourse of the End of the Lord's Supper," in *The Complete Works of Stephen Charnock* (1864–1866; repr., Edinburgh: Banner of Truth, 1985), 4:407.

2. Charnock, "End of the Lord's Supper," 4:408.

3. Joachim Jeremias, *The Eucharistic Words of Jesus* (London: SCM, 1987), 224.

4. Jeremias, *Eucharistic Words of Jesus*, 253.

5. Matthew Poole, *A Commentary on the Holy Bible* (London: Banner of Truth, 1969), 3:127.

6. John Newton, "May the Grace of Christ Our Savior," 1779.

Chapter 17

1. For more on these themes, see G. K. Beale, *The Temple and the Church's Mission: A Biblical Theology of the Dwelling Place of God*, New Studies in Biblical Theology 15 (Downers Grove, IL: IVP Academic, 2004).

2. J. Petit-Senn, in *Forty Thousand Sublime and Beautiful Thoughts Gathered from the Roses, Clover Blossoms, Geraniums, Violets, Morning-Glories, and Pansies of Literature*, compiled by Charles Noel Douglas (New York: Christian Herald, 1915), 940.

3. Herman Bavinck, *Reformed Dogmatics*, vol. 4, *Holy Spirit, Church and New Creation*, ed. John Bolt, trans. John Vriend (Grand Rapids, MI: Baker Academic, 2008), 640.

4. Richard Baxter, *The Christian's Companion in Solitude* (Glasgow: William Collins, 1827), 269.

5. Jonathan Edwards, *The Works of Jonathan Edwards*, vol. 13, *The "Miscellanies," a–500*, ed. Thomas A. Schafer (New Haven, CT: Yale University Press, 1994), 275–76.

6. John Lennon, "Imagine," 1971.

7. This eulogy was written on the flyleaf (blank page) of Walton's copy of Sibbes's *Returning Backslider* (1650). See Jessica Martin, *Walton's Lives: Conformist Commemorations and the Rise of Biography* (Oxford: Oxford University Press, 2001), 279.

Chapter 18

1. Parts of this section are adapted from Mark Jones, "Hell's Horrors vs. Heaven's Happiness (Updated)," *Reformation21* (blog), Alliance of Confessing Evangelicals, May 4, 2015, http://www.reformation21.org /blog/2015/05/hells-horrors-vs-heavens-happi.php. Used by permission of the Alliance of Confessing Evangelicals.

2. John Calvin, *Institutes of the Christian Religion*, ed. John T. McNeill, trans. Ford Lewis Battles (Louisville: Westminster John Knox, 2008), 3.25.12.

3. Quoted in Sinclair Ferguson, "Pastoral Theology: The Preacher and Hell," in *Hell under Fire: Modern Scholarship Reinvents Eternal Punishment*, ed. Robert A. Peterson and Christopher W. Morgan (Grand Rapids, MI: Zondervan, 2004), 34.

General Index

Scripture Index

Also Available from Mark Jones

For more information, visit **crossway.org**.